sto

WILD CATS

Probably the most popular of all the animals in the zoo are the big cats and their relatives. This book is a general account of all the living species and their habits. Besides descriptions of the cats and their natural environments, ways in which man has used these animals are also described, such as hunting with cheetahs and tiger-hunting using elephants. The cat family is introduced with its ancestors, including saber-toothed 'tigers,' and is followed through its various developments to the wild cats we know today.

A GROSSET ALL-COLOR GUIDE

WILD CATS

BY MICHAEL BOORER
Illustrated by Peter Warner

GROSSET & DUNLAP
A NATIONAL GENERAL COMPANY
Publishers • New York

Copyright © 1970 by Grosset & Dunlap, Inc.
All Rights Reserved
Published Simultaneously in Canada
Copyright © 1969 by The Hamlyn Publishing Group Ltd.
Library of Congress Catalog Card No.: 79-120432
Printed in the United States of America

1549281

CONTENTS

INTRODUCTION

The Cats—Fiercest of Hunters

No one is indifferent to cats. People either love them or hate them. If questioned about his feelings, the average cat-lover would probably talk of the graceful movements and the endearing and friendly, yet independent ways of the domestic cat, but this is only part of the story. It is only necessary to visit a lion house in any zoo to see that most people also find wild cats fascinating and that these cats are by no means friendly. If most are graceful, some, such as the jaguar, are clumsy by comparison. That another explanation exists becomes very clear when the excited crowd throngs around the lion's cage at feeding time. The fascination that cats exert has a great deal to do with the fact that they are meat eaters, or carnivores.

Only plants manufacture food from simple raw materials: water and carbon dioxide from the air are combined through the energy of sunlight into sugar and other complex food molecules. Once this has been done, animals obtain their food by eating plants. But soon after the origin of simple plants and plant-eating animals some 2½ billion years ago—there was an alternative. Some animals could now feed on other animals. The carnivorous way of life is therefore almost as old as life on this planet. As the herbivorous or plant-eating animals have developed defenses, the carnivores in their turn have developed more efficient weapons and hunting methods.

Animals with backbones first evolved where life began—in the sea. Being larger and more active than most other animals they became successful. During the past few hundred million years some fishes invaded the land as the first amphibians, some of which later became reptiles. These animals all had cold blood, which was adequate for an aquatic life, but not ideal for active life in varied climates on land. The warm-blooded mammals evolved from the reptiles, and within the last 70 million years they have become the most important active land animals.

Like all other animals, the mammals show a range of specializations. Some of them are herbivorous and others are hunters. There are other carnivorous mammals, but the real specialists are the members of the order Carnivora. The most

4

Two extremes of the cat family—the lion and the domestic cat.

highly developed of these, in a sense the pinnacle of mammalian carnivore evolution, are the cats.

In the same way, the hunting methods of the cats are highly developed. Most cats hunt by stealth, creeping up on their prey unobserved, and then pouncing rapidly on their victims. This behavior can be observed in domestic cats, as they lie in wait in the garden for mice or birds. The cheetah hunts more like a dog, running swiftly after its prey. But whatever the method, the cat's perfect coordination of mind and limb makes it a successful hunter. Hunting is always an exciting subject, and perfection must demand respect. No wonder that man, himself a mammal, finds the cats—from the tabby to the lion—fascinating.

5

EVOLUTION OF THE CAT

The Origin of the Carnivora

Like many other groups of living mammals, the Carnivora are descended from small, furry, insect-eating animals that flourished about 70 million years ago. Some descendants of this group, such as the shrews, have changed very little while others, including the hoofed herbivorous mammals and man himself, have changed a great deal. The Carnivora, too, have undergone considerable change, but in a very understandable way.

The first really successful group of animals within the order Carnivora flourished between 40 and 50 million years ago. We know this because their fossilized remains are common in rocks formed at that time. The creodonts, as this early group are called, have been extinct for millions of years, but we know that they were once successful because a whole range of them existed, adapted for a number of different carnivorous modes of life.

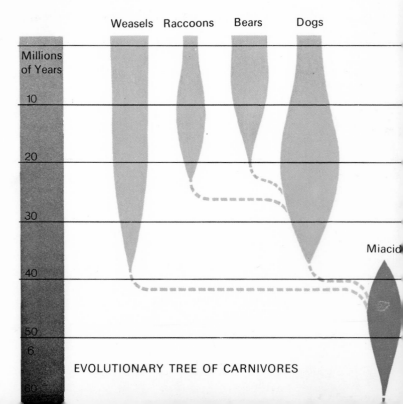

EVOLUTIONARY TREE OF CARNIVORES

The earliest of them were quite small—about the size of a weasel—and had very small brains. None of the teeth in either the upper or the lower jaw were enlarged for the purpose of shearing through meat. Their bodies and limbs were slender, and they moved on flat feet with their heels touching the ground as they walked.

From these early creodonts a host of more highly developed animals evolved. These animals had as shearing teeth the first or second upper molars and the second or third lower molars. Exactly which teeth were used for this purpose may seem unimportant, but small details can be important in science. Shearing teeth have also been developed by the modern successful carnivores, but in a slightly different part of the jaw.

At the height of their success the creodonts included medium-sized, wolf-like animals, and huge bear-like creatures, but by 10 million years ago the last lingering line of them had died out. The descendants of the miacids, another early group within the Carnivora, had come to rule the roost.

Cats   Mongooses   Hyenas   Sealions   Seals   Walruses

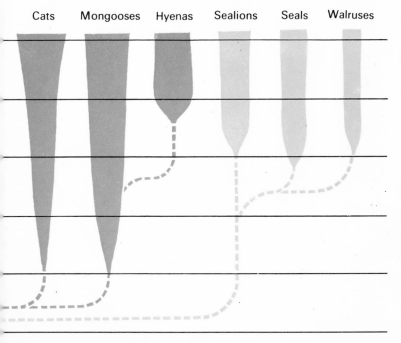

A miacid, a prehistoric forebear of the cats.

The Beginnings of the Modern Carnivora

The miacids sprang from the same stock as the creodonts. At first they were overshadowed by their more numerous cousins, although they flourished as forest-dwellers, climbing easily and often hunting among the branches of trees. As befits climbers they were not large, being perhaps the size of a small cat. They had long bodies and tails, and short but flexible limbs. Each foot bore five toes which were probably armed with retractile claws, not unlike those of modern cats. Their brains were larger than those of the creodonts and, significantly, the shearing teeth they developed were formed from the last premolar tooth of the upper jaw and the first molar of the lower.

About 40 million years ago, a time when the creodonts were dwindling, a whole range of hunters of different kinds were evolving from the miacid stock. At this time the groups which we know today as the families of modern Carnivora became recognizable. The miacids themselves died out, but their more highly developed descendants grew in numbers and importance as they adopted the modes of life left vacant by the creodonts.

Marine Carnivores

One surpising development was the evolution, from normal land animals, of a group of excellent swimmers capable of spending much of their time at sea. Seals, sea lions and walruses used to be grouped together under the name pinnipeds ('fin-footed'). New research indicates, however, that the seals were derived from otter-like weasels, while the sea lions and walruses descended from bears. In all tails became shorter and limbs became powerfully webbed for swimming. They kept their fur, but as wet fur is useless for heat retention, the fat beneath the skin became the most important means of keeping the body warm. Today there are several groups of aquatic carnivores.

The Sea Lions still retain the ear-flaps typical of mammals and swim mainly by using their long forelimbs. Out of the water they can use their hind feet to move in a clumsy gallop.
The Walruses lack ear-flaps and move clumsily on land or in water. They feed on shellfish and have teeth that are adapted for this purpose. They are an offshoot of the eared seals.
The Seals are the most aquatic of the carnivores. They lack ear-flaps and swim well using their hind feet, which are of no use out of water. Like the sea lions, most of them feed on fish and have sharply pointed teeth.

Sea lions evolved from the same miacid stock as did the cats. Both in their different ways are fierce and able hunters.

The remaining modern Carnivora are known as the fissipeds—a name which means 'split-footed ones' and refers to the fact that they do not have webbed feet. As the majority of the Carnivora are fissipeds it is most convenient to classify them into two main groups.

The Dog-like Group of Families

The oldest of the fissipeds are closer to the dogs than they are to the cats. These carnivores have retained the long jaw of the miacids and have a relatively large number of teeth. It might appear that numerous teeth ought to be an asset to a hunter, but this is not so. A long jaw does not bite as hard as a short jaw and, as long as there are enough teeth left to do the job, a short jaw is therefore best. However, the dog-like carnivores have one advantage. Above their long mouths they have room for large and most efficient noses. Their sense of smell is unequalled. There are four families in this group:

The Brown Bear, like the cats, is descended from the miacids and has their long jaw and large number of teeth.

The Dog Family consists of running hunters, always moving on tiptoe, such as wolves and foxes.

The Bear Family contains a few heavyweight, flat-footed species.

The Raccoon Family, like the bears, consist of flat-footed animals, but being smaller, they are mostly excellent climbers.

The Weasel Family has retained something of the original miacid shape, but its members—martens, otters and skunks—have a wide range of hunting methods.

Other descendants of the miacids include the raccoon (*top*), the marten (*center*), which resembles a miacid more than other dog-like mammals, and the wolf (*bottom*).

The Indian Mongoose, like the cat, is an agile hunter and is known for its practice of killing snakes.

The Cat-like Group of Families

Apart from the cats themselves, two other families of the Carnivora have short jaws and hence improved biting power. **The Mongoose and Civet Family** contains many species which have a superficial resemblance to the weasels. This resemblance exists partly because both families have retained something of the appearance of the miacid ancestors they share, but mainly because some members of each family have separately become adapted for the same forms of hunting. Mongooses and weasels rarely compete for the same food, however, for most weasels come from the cool climates of Europe, northern Asia and North America, while mongooses typically inhabit the warmer parts of Asia and Africa.

The mongoose family contains about eighty different species. Some of them, like the Indian Mongoose, are fierce hunters, capable of working through quick cover and diving into burrows, but others, such as the equally short-legged Meerkat of Africa, feed mainly on insects and eat quite a lot of plant food as well. The genets and civets have slightly longer legs and are more cat-like in appearance. They are expert climbers, and various species inhabit the forests of Africa and Asia feeding on small mammals and birds, as well as invertebrates and fruit.

The Hyena Family contains only four species. At a quick glance the hyenas look more like dogs than cats, but with their weak-looking, sloping backs they could never undertake the strenuous running and hunting typical of the dogs, and neither do they need to. With their shorter jaws the hyenas have, in relation to their size, a more powerful bite than any other living mammal, and for this reason they rarely lack food. Once the lion has killed its prey, and the vultures and such mammalian scavengers as the jackals have eaten their fill, then there is always food for the hyena. Coming last to the banquet, they are able to crack bones which no other mammal can deal with, and are thus able to dine on bone marrow. This is the mode of life of both the Striped Hyena of Africa and Asia and the bigger Spotted Hyena of East Africa.

The other two species are less formidable. The Brown Hyena of southern Africa mainly feeds on carrion which it finds on seashores, while the aardwolf of eastern and southern Africa has unusually weak jaws and eats insects.

The Striped Hyena of Africa and Asia. Although it resembles a dog, it is closely related to the cat.

Cats of the Past

The first cats were descended from the same ancestors as the mongooses and civets, but 35 million years ago the cats were clearly distinguishable as a distinct type. Perhaps it would be better to say two types for right from the beginning, there were two types of cat, not one, and this state of affairs lasted until only a few thousand years ago. One of these lines became adapted for hunting active animals, and this stock eventually gave rise to all of the cats we know today. The other line, successful until times which must be regarded as recent when considered against the long perspective of geological time, consisted of the saber-tooths, often mistakenly called 'tigers'.

All the Carnivora have well-developed canine teeth, but in the saber-tooths these weapons became phenomenal. Even the early forms, which were cats of medium size, had remarkably large canines, but the trend reached its peak in the Saber-toothed 'Tiger' (*Smilodon*), which was as large as a tiger and had fangs seven or eight inches in length.

It is always difficult to be sure exactly how extinct animals lived, for we know them only as fossils and a certain amount of guesswork is involved. However, almost certainly the saber-tooths were adapted to hunt animals such as rhinoceroses and elephants, whose chief defenses were their size and their thick skins. The Saber-Toothed 'Tiger' could open its mouth very widely, so that the teeth were exposed for use like daggers, and inflict a slashing, stabbing wound even upon the most thick-skinned of prey.

Saber-tooths mostly inhabited the northern hemisphere— North America, Europe and Asia—but at one stage within the past million years they also invaded South America, a continent which has been cut off by the sea, and therefore difficult for land animals to reach, for most of its history. While the mammoths and the mastodons flourished, so did the saber-tooths that hunted them. When the giant land mammals dwindled in numbers the saber-tooths died out. They were specialists, creatures unable to adopt other forms of hunting.

Their cousins, the ancestors of the modern cats, lived on. Chance plays a large part in these matters, and by chance they had not blundered into an evolutionary cul-de-sac.

Saber-Toothed 'Tigers' had fangs seven or eight inches long, and the shape of the skull (*below*) enabled them to open their mouths very widely. The normal jaw muscles were not especially large, so that the strength of the bite itself could have been nothing remarkable. The muscles of the neck, however, were very strong so that the whole head, with the jaws gaping, could be jerked powerfully downward. In this way, a savage wound was inflicted on the prey.

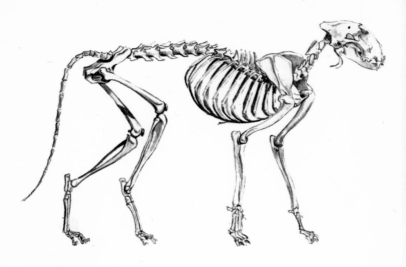

THE CAT'S BODY

Modern Cats

Even before the remarkable killing spree in which man has indulged during the past few hundred years, there were far more kinds of animals extinct than still living. At any stage in the history of life on earth the species alive were the lucky survivors from times past—lucky because they were adapted to conditions that still continued to exist. The modern cats are stealthy hunters, capable of sudden bursts of power. This is what they are adapted for from the front of their short jaws to the sharp ends of their claws.

Cats hunt animals which are wary and which are well able to escape if they perceive danger. A stealthy, silent approach is essential, and for this a cat must have a supple and freely moving body. Once within range—and cats of most kinds get very close before launching the final attack—stealth is abandoned and speed replaces it. Over the last few feet or yards the cat pounces. Over slightly longer distances a cat may sprint for a few strides, but cats never run while hunting in the way that wild dogs such as wolves do. An exception is the cheetah, which will often launch itself at full speed in pursuit of its prey, rather in the way that dogs hunt.

Cat-style hunting calls for a strong but flexible body, yet

The cat's skeleton (*left*) has a flexible backbone and leg bones connected to powerful muscles (*above*), enabling the animal to spring and move with agility.

no great powers of endurance. Basically, the only parts of the skeleton which have changed greatly from the original shrew-like mammal pattern in the course of evolution are the skull (including the teeth) and, to a slightly lesser degree, the limbs. The backbone is very flexible, especially in the lumbar (or waist) region, and it is from the back, together with the hind legs, which can be bent and then straightened in a strong kick, that the cats derive their power in pouncing. The ease with which the legs can move, even in a crouching position, is due to their ability to bend freely at the shoulder, elbow, wrist, knee and ankle, and this explains the skill with which a cat creeps toward its prey.

Graceful movement calls for a well-developed system of muscles, for the best of skeletons is useless without muscle to power it, and this cats certainly possess. The grace with which they move is proverbial. As might be expected, the strongest muscles are to be found in the lumbar region and hind legs (for springing) and the shoulder region and neck (for power in striking), but it is only necessary to watch a kitten playing with a ping-pong ball to see that cats are capable of delicate movements as well.

The Limbs

The first mammals had *plantigrade* limbs—that is to say that they walked on flat feet with the wrist and heel making contact with the ground during each stride. This form of limb was ideal for a small mammal clambering about among vegetation which was large in relation to its size. The flat part of the foot could make contact with the rounded plant stem, giving an efficient grip. Some mammals have retained this sort of limb because they are still climbers. Examples are the monkeys and their relation, man. Other mammals, like the bears, retain plantigrade limbs because they are useful in spreading the animal's heavy weight over the ground.

But this type of limb is not perfect for all purposes. We are plantigrade when we walk, but when we run we rise on tiptoe to effectively make the legs longer so that we can travel farther with each stride. Where running or springing are important, animals become adapted to move in this way all the time. Because such animals move on their toes, or digits, they are said to have *digitigrade* limbs. Cats are digitigrade.

To understand the cat's limbs in relation to our own it is only necessary to appreciate that the bend which appears to be in the position of a knee in a cat's hind leg, but which

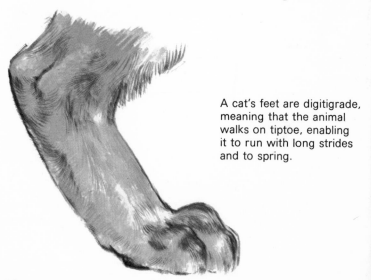

A cat's feet are digitigrade, meaning that the animal walks on tiptoe, enabling it to run with long strides and to spring.

A cat's claws are retractile and are drawn into the openings in the feet when they are not being used.

bends the same way as the human ankle really *is* an ankle. The soft pads upon which the hunting cat can move so quietly are not on the sole of the foot, but are on the toes or at the base of them.

Cats have five toes on their front feet. The digit which corresponds to the human thumb is shorter than the others but is useful when the forelimb is used for manipulation. On the hind foot there are only four toes, the digit corresponding to the human big toe being absent.

The limbs of vertebrates normally end in claws and have done so almost ever since limbs evolved on the first amphibians. Almost certainly the original function of claws was to protect the ends of the digits from wear. Claws were adapted to take the wear, growing as fast as they were worn away. However, once structures have come into existence they often acquire new functions and this is true of the claws of many animals. Cats' claws have developed to become so useful in other ways that they are now useless for their original purpose.

Cats have retractile claws. This means that the claws are normally hidden in special openings on the ends of the digits. Thus, when a cat walks the claws do not scrape on the ground, which is a great advantage during stealthy movement. Because the claws are retracted they remain sharp until they are really needed, when they can be pulled out by special muscles and be ready for action. Sharp claws make excellent weapons and are also useful for climbing trees. Most cats climb well.

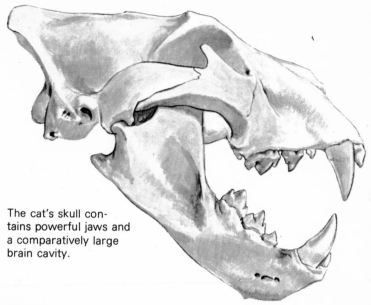

The cat's skull contains powerful jaws and a comparatively large brain cavity.

The Head

As is the case in most animals, invertebrate or vertebrate, the head of a cat contains several of the most important sense organs: the brain which is, in a sense, the chief information and executive center of the body, and also the mouth. Cats require keen senses to detect the tiny clues that may be useful to a hunter, and the eyes, ears and nose of a cat are all large and very highly developed.

As a group the mammals are the most intelligent animals in existence. The cats are not the most intelligent of mammals—that place is reserved for man and his closest relations—but compared to the mammals as a whole the cats must be regarded as reasonably bright. Their brains and, in particular, their cerebral hemispheres, which have to do with intelligent behavior, are large.

Nevertheless much of their behavior is not the product of reason, but of instinct. Instinctive behavior is automatic, inborn behavior which happens as a result of the way in which the nerve messages pass through fixed circuits by way of the brain to the muscles or glands, which are responsible for activity. Once a certain group of circumstances occurs, an appropriate response is made without pause for cogitation.

Behavior of this kind, although rather inflexible, is adequate for most of the situations that a cat encounters.

The Jaws and Teeth

As we have seen, the jaws of a cat are short, and this makes for power in biting. The large muscles which power the jaws extend from the lower jaw itself and, passing over the sides of the head, are joined to the roof of the skull where there is a bony ridge ideal for the purpose.

Mammals are unique in having various types of teeth in different parts of their mouths. At the front are the incisors, which are often chisel-shaped as they are in man, although those of the Carnivora are more pointed. Immediately behind these teeth come the sharply pointed eye teeth or canines. The teeth at the sides of the mouth are sometimes grouped together as cheek teeth, but are of two types. Those immediately behind the canines are the premolars, and these are usually simpler in structure than the molars that come behind them. A mammal has two sets of teeth during its lifetime—the milk teeth, which are lost quite early, and the adult teeth. The milk teeth do not form a complete set as molars are never present at this stage. The molars in all mammals only come in as part of the adult set.

Different kinds of mammals have not only teeth of different shapes, adapted according to their diet, but also different numbers of teeth of the various kinds. The number of teeth typically possessed by a species is conveniently expressed in a dental formula. This gives, for one side of the jaws only, the numbers of teeth of each type present, figures for the upper and lower jaws being given separately. Thus the dental formula of the cats, which altogether have six incisors in the upper jaw (three on each side), and six more below, one canine on each side in both the upper and lower jaws, three premolars on each side of the upper jaw and two below, and one molar on each side above and below is:

$$I\frac{3}{3} C\frac{1}{1} P\frac{3}{2} M\frac{1}{1}$$

This means that there is a total of thirty teeth altogether in the full adult set.

The first of the premolars of the upper jaw is small and

may in some cases be absent. As is the case in all of the modern Carnivora, the hindmost of the upper premolars and the first of the lower molars (and the only lower molar in the case of the cats) are large. These teeth, known as the carnassials, are of great importance in shearing through meat.

The shortening of the jaw typical of the cats and their closer relatives goes together with a reduction in the number of cheek teeth. As a comparison, the dogs have the dental formula:

$$I\frac{3}{3}C\frac{1}{1}P\frac{4}{4}M\frac{2}{3}$$

The cat's incisor teeth are of little importance in hunting or feeding, although they are sometimes used to nibble small tidbits from a carcass. The rasping action of the rough tongue is more important in this respect, however. The incisors are more often used for grooming the fur, the upper lip being curled back to expose them for this purpose.

The canines are of great importance for they, together with the claws, are the weapons used in making a kill. They are in use again immediately afterwards, ripping and tearing at the prey so as to reduce the feast to manageable proportions. Once this has been accomplished the carnassial teeth come into play.

Cats have large, grinning mouths, and because of this it is

easy for them to use the teeth at the sides of their mouths in feeding. The meat is taken between the crowns of the carnassial teeth which, as the lower jaw moves straight upward, approach and pass close to each other like the blades of a pair of shears, cutting through the food. Once this has been done the morsel in the mouth is swallowed at once. Cats have no teeth suitable for grinding food, and in any case meat is easy to digest and does not need to be pulverized first.

Cat's teeth are ideal for their purpose, but if used in other ways would be almost useless, as anyone who has ever watched a cat trying to take a morning snack of grass (presumably for health reasons) will know.

A cat bites its food in various ways. The front *canine* teeth act like a pair of daggers (*left*) to kill and tear the prey. The side *carnassial* teeth act with a shearing action (*right*) to cut through pieces of meat, which are then swallowed whole.

At night, a cat's pupils
open wide.

The Eyes

A cat's eyes are on the front of the head rather than at the
side. This means that cats do not have all-round vision, a
feature which would not be important to them for they are
fierce enough not to fear surprise attacks. But they are able
to judge distance, an ability which is important when
pouncing on other animals who will not allow a second
attempt if it can be avoided. Like most other mammals, cats
are color blind and do not see in such sharp detail as human
beings do. Nevertheless, their eyesight is good when compared to that of almost any mammal other than man.

The night vision of cats is proverbial. In fact not all kinds
of cats have equally good vision in this respect, and none
of them equal mammals like the bushbabies, which are completely nocturnal animals.

Cats of many species are adapted to hunt both by day and

by night as opportunity offers, and the design of the eyes is therefore a compromise. The most obvious sign of this adaptation appears in the shape of the pupils. In the domestic cat and many other species the pupil is not round, but forms a vertical slit. A pupil of this shape can be opened more widely and closed more narrowly than a pupil of the conventional round shape, and is therefore more useful in an eye which must work under a wide variety of light. A vertical slit is of more use than a horizontal one because in bright light the amount of light entering the eye is still further reduced when the eyelids are partly closed, thus reducing the functional part of the pupil slit to a mere pinpoint.

Because their eyes glow at night, cats were regarded as sacred by the ancient Egyptians. The cat, it was thought, has eyes which reflect the sun when it is hidden from mere man. The true explanation is only a little less remarkable. Beneath the sensitive nerve cells inside a cat's eye there is a reflecting layer, so that in dim light each ray of light has two chances of affecting the nerve cells, one on the way into the eye and the other on the way out again.

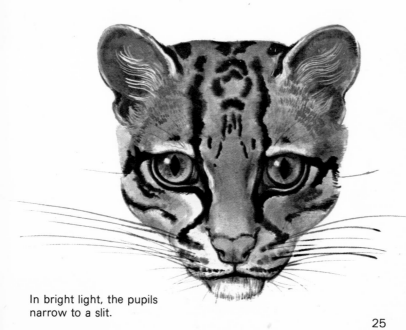

In bright light, the pupils narrow to a slit.

The Ears

The ears of a cat are even larger than they appear to be at first, for the fur growing round their base conceals their true size. They are, in fact, huge ear-trumpets and serve to funnel even tiny sounds into the internal ears, from which the information passes to the brain. The external ears are also useful in locating the source of the sound, and this is partly explained by the fact that they can be moved on the head, swivelling around like direction-finders until they point in the direction in which the sound is loudest. In general, cats have the largest ears possible, bearing in mind that there are other factors involved.

Large ears, although efficient, can have disadvantages. For example, extremely long ears might be damaged by prickly undergrowth and would be a mixed blessing to a cat which inhabits dense bush country. A more important

An example of Allen's Rule among the cats.
The marbled cat living in a warm climate has
longer ears than the cold adapted snow
leopard.

consideration, however, has to do with temperature. We ourselves know only too well that on chilly days our ears quickly become cold. This is because they are well shaped for losing heat; flat, thin structures have a large surface through which heat can be lost. Despite their thin covering of fur, a cat's ears are liable to get cold almost as much as human ears.

For this reason the size of the ears found on a species of cat depends in part upon the climate in which the species lives. Cats from warm places, such as the marbled cat, have relatively large ears, while the snow leopard, which inhabits cold mountainous parts of central Asia, has relatively small ears.

Of course, the climate does not only affect cats' ears. Any flattened and long, thin appendages on the bodies of all warm-blooded animals will be equally affected. A rough, but more or less accurate summary of the situation is made by Allen's Rule, which states that species or varieties from cool climates will, in general, tend to have smaller appendages than will related species from warmer climates. If a smaller organ would not, for one reason or another, be good enough for the task for which it is required another answer must be found. This is the main reason why Allen's Rule is not always accurate. It is not only a snow leopard's ears which will feel the cold; the long tail will also be subject to frostbite. However, although a shorter tail would be easier to keep warm it apparently would not be of much use to the animal for some other important function. Thus snow leopards have very long tails which are, however, covered with remarkably long, thick fur.

The Nose

It is sometimes said that cats have no sense of smell, but this is most certainly untrue. Like most mammals, they have very efficient noses. However, it is true that they have smaller noses and a less perfect sense of smell than their distant cousins, the wild dogs. This is understandable, for wolves mainly hunt by scent, running tirelessly for mile after mile with nothing to guide them but the scent of their quarry, until at last they begin to catch up with it. Cats locate their prey by means of sight, sound or smell, and stalk by sight.

Special glands evolved for the purpose of secreting scents exist in all cat species. These odors serve as aids in various social relationships, particularly at mating time.

The Whiskers

Whiskers, or *vibrissae* to give them their technical name, are simple large, specially adapted hairs. But while the function of ordinary mammalian hair is to trap a blanket of air and thus conserve heat, cat whiskers are useful for another purpose.

They are dead, of course. All hairs are. A hair consists of a dead rod of a substance called *keratin* which is produced by a living root. But although hair is dead tissue, if it is touched it passes on the pressure, and this can be picked up by living nerve endings in the skin. This is true of all hairs, but it is especially true of whiskers. They are extra strong and have a large number of nerves clustered around their

A leopard's snout is shorter than that of a wolf, which has a better sense of smell.

A cat's whiskers help it to find its way in very dim light.

roots. Above all, they are situated on the head of the animal, and on a four-legged animal which moves head first this is the most useful place to have extra organs of touch.

Stories about domestic cats using their whiskers as a sort of gauge, used to test gaps to see if they are wide enough for the body to pass through, are untrue. One has only to look at some overfed pets to see that the idea is laughable. Nevertheless, when moving in dim light—even with specially adapted eyes—the sense of touch can be valuable, performing the same sort of service that a walking stick does for a blind man.

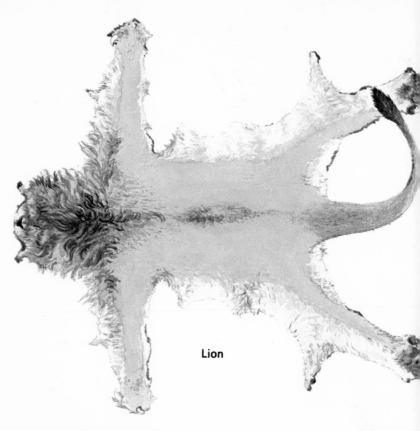

Lion

The Fur and Markings

Cats of all kinds have beautiful coats. Naturally, the fur is
longest in those species which live in cool climates, but
even tropical cats are well wrapped up. In the tropics it can
be cold at night.

A stealthy hunter must be able to approach its prey unseen, and the most important function of the coat color is
to provide camouflage. Cats that hunt in the open, as lions
do, are therefore brownish to match their surroundings,
while cats which keep to thicker cover have patterns of
spots or stripes which blend with the shadows cast by the
leaves.

Not all of a cat's markings have to do with camouflage.
Some are concerned with making the animal's signalling
systems more efficient, such as dark tassels on lions' tails.

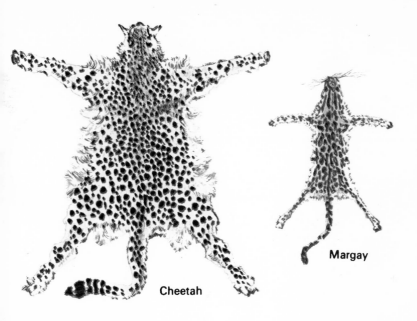

Cheetah

Margay

The markings of a wild cat may provide camouflage or improve social signals.

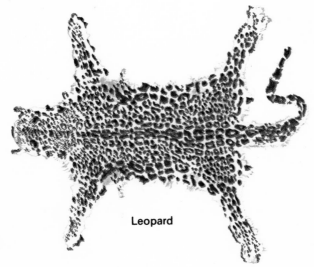

Leopard

CAT BEHAVIOR

Territory

Like the cat in *The Jungle Book* who 'walked by himself', cats are solitary creatures on the whole. The reason for this is obvious enough. It suits their way of getting a living. For success in hunting, a cat must be able to get really close to its prey without being observed, and surprise is much more easily achieved if the hunter works on his own.

There is also another reason for the cat's unsociable ways. In the wild, hunters can never be as common as the animals they feed on. If they were they would soon run out of food and starve. Cats therefore tend to space themselves out, each one defending an area—called a *territory*—that is big enough to support it. Each animal gets to know its own territory, with the advantage that on its home ground an animal is never at a loss when it comes to finding anything it needs for survival.

The territories of different individuals of the same species do not overlap, but around each territory there may be a neutral area, known as the home range, where neighbors can meet on more or less equal terms. Territorial defense may take the form of fighting, but more often bluff is sufficient.

The pattern of territorial behavior described so far is common to many animals. How far it applies to wild cats is far from clear. Wild cats are furtive by nature, and the difficulty of studying the movements and behavior of, say, an ocelot in its native jungles will be apparent. Such observations as have been made are sketchy and do not form a clear picture. However, domestic cats are easier to watch, and recent observations of this species are of great interest.

For much of the time domestic cats behave as territorial animals, keeping apart as each individual stalks around its own territory, keeping to favored paths along the tops of garden walls or through shrubberies. However, sometimes this pattern breaks down, and the proprietors of several adjoining territories congregate together. This is a form of social behavior, even if vocal exchanges do sound distinctly unfriendly when heard through a bedroom window.

Lions and Tigers

The idea that typical cat behavior includes both solitary and social phases may be of value in interpreting the known facts about the behavior of the big cats.

Lions are quite closely related to the other big cats. In zoos, for example, they can cross-breed with tigers. Nevertheless, at first sight the behavior of these two species appears to be very different. Large gatherings of tigers are unknown, but lions, in part of their range at least, are the only cats which normally live together in social groups at all times. Only for the lions is there a special name for a group, and we speak of a *pride* of lions.

Behavior, like any other feature of an animal, is adaptive and aids survival. Like the form of the body itself, it is derived through combination and reconstruction of its ancestors' heredities. If the ancestors which both lions and tigers share were both solitary and social at different times then, by varying modifications of this pattern, the behavior of the different kinds of modern big cats could come into being.

The tiger's behavior has probably changed least in the course of evolution. They hunt in thick cover—the traditional hunting-ground of the cats, in fact—and have continued to be solitary for most of this time. Whether their normal behavior also includes an occasional social gathering is not clear. Their social instincts may have become reduced in the course of time, but men who have made a point of stalking wild tigers have usually not had scientific observation in mind, being more concerned with their own predatory instincts.

How lions behave depends upon where they live. In western Africa, where lions are no longer common, there were never the large herds of game which occurred in other parts of the continent. The lions which lived there stalked single animals, and solitary behavior was best for this purpose. In eastern and southern Africa, on the other hand, the lions' prey lives in herds, and these are very difficult for a single lion to approach. Collectively, a herd has many eyes, ears and nostrils, and for a predator to approach undetected by one of these keen sense organs is impossible. Under these conditions, the lions must use teamwork to overcome the vigilance of their prey, and the social aspects of the lions' behavior have perhaps become exaggerated.

Lions live together in groups, or *prides,* in eastern and southern Africa. They help each other in hunting the herds of animals on which they prey.

Social Signals

All animals need some sort of language. Not a complicated one like English or Chinese—these human languages are a by-product of intelligence and we have to learn them. But there is a basic human language which all men speak. A smile or a scream of fear can be understood by an American as well as a Chinese man. The ability to understand communication at this level is born in us. It is at this instinctive level that the communication systems of other animal species operate.

Notice that the basic human language does not only consist of sounds. We can also make faces and if the mouth moves, as it does when we smile, then this signal is the more obvious if our lips are naturally pink and our teeth are white. Moving a part of the body—it does not have to be the face— is as useful a form of signalling as any other if the species concerned has sharp eyesight. If the human sense of smell was better we should make more use of scent in signalling. Most mammal species do. Signals which can be heard, seen or smelled can all play a part.

As we have already seen, cats make use of scent signals, but we are far from sure exactly what this part of their vocabulary means to them. It is difficult for us to appreciate the subtleties of smells.

Cats also use sounds. They roar, yowl, spit and miaow. All cats purr to show that they are pleased. Small differences occur. The big cats—the lion, tiger, leopard, jaguar and snow leopard—all roar, while the smaller cats have more high-pitched voices. The big cats pause for breath between each purr, but the small cats purr almost continuously.

Cats also use visual signals. They wave their tails as a sign of unpleasurable exictement. Stripes, or in the case of the lion a tassel, on the tail make this signal more obvious. This is a very deep-rooted signal among the Carnivora. Dogs wag their tails as a sign of excitement which is usually pleasurable, but the theme of excitement is common to both groups. Even with dogs one can never be quite sure that pleasure is the emotion involved—excitement is the only certain feature. This may be why people are sometimes bitten by 'treacherous' dogs that were wagging their tails at the time.

A cat's ears are among its most effective signals. If they are laid back then one mood is indicated, but if they are right forward, and especially if the teeth are exposed in a snarl at the same time, this indicates quite another frame of mind. The big cats have special markings on the backs of their ears to emphasize these signals, but all cats use the ears in this way. The lynxes have long tassels of hair on their ears. This may be because they have short tails and must be able to compensate for their lack of ability to signal with the tail.

A cat's ears are particularly indicative of its moods. These can easily be seen in a domestic cat. When it is contented and lying still, the ears are usually laid back. But if the animal's attention is attracted by calling to it, the ears will rise up in awareness. The same kind of social signals may be observed in wild cats such as tigers (*above*).

Cats in Nature

The part played by predators such as the cats in maintaining the balance of nature may appear to be a purely destructive one, but in fact this is not the case. They are not simply destroyers, but play a vital part in maintaining a balance. Without them the very species that they hunt would be worse off, paradoxical though this may be.

Animal food begins with plants. Any given area, with its climate and its soil, can support a certain amount of plant life. The plants will grow and, over the years, the type of vegetation may tend to change—from grassland to bushy scrub and then to forest, for example—but this does not always happen, because plant growth is kept in check by the herbivorous animals that consume the increase in plants.

As a result of the food they eat, the herbivores in their turn thrive, grow and breed. Breeding will tend to increase their numbers, and this will mean that there are more mouths to be fed. Soon a situation could easily arise in which the plants are eaten faster than they can grow, so that the whole area becomes a denuded desert. That this does not happen is entirely due to hunters like the wild cats.

Predatory animals must kill off just enough of the herbivores to keep the population steady. This is not achieved by accident. If there are too many hunters their prey will become scarce and some of them may starve. If there are too few hunters then hunting will be easy, and the hunters will breed well, building up their numbers. The balance is a delicate one but, although there are bound to be minor fluctuations in animal populations due to disease and such natural disasters as bush fires and locusts, on the whole a balance is achieved over the years.

The carnivores are thus at the top of a pyramid of life with the more numerous herbivores upon which they feed below them and the still more numerous plants at the base. Food passes from the bottom to the top. The actual numbers concerned are bound to vary with the conditions, but in one count made in the African grassland, for every lion that was counted, there were well over a hundred herbivorous mammals of the kind that provide lions with food.

Man, depending on the kind of interference he undertakes, strongly influences, for good or bad, this balance of nature.

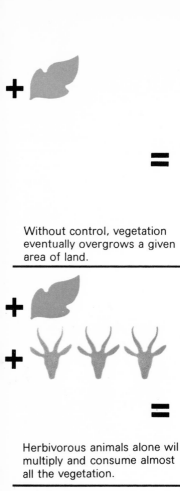

Without control, vegetation eventually overgrows a given area of land.

Herbivorous animals alone wil multiply and consume almost all the vegetation.

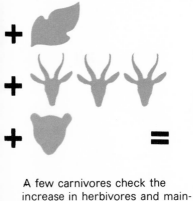

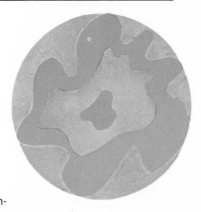

A few carnivores check the increase in herbivores and maintain a balance.

Conservation

During most of his million years or so of existence, man has killed other animals whenever the opportunity was presented. He has mostly been a hunter like any other, and the effects of his hunting were not unduly severe. Within the last few hundred years, however, a change has taken place. Man has produced firearms which make hunting much easier. Animals which would previously have escaped have been slaughtered in the millions.

Man's technical triumphs have also had other effects. The spread of agriculture has meant that there is less room for wild animals. The elimination of disease from man's domesticated herds of cattle has sometimes meant that the wild animals, which also harbor the disease, must be slain. All over the world the large stocks of wild animals have dwindled, as man has sought more and more to control his environment.

Almost too late man has come to realize the danger. If the untimely extinction of many species is not to occur, special reserves must be set up where wild animals can survive unmolested.

In nature reserves, game wardens keep an eye on wild cats and other animals to make sure that the balance of nature is being conserved.

To be truly successful, a game reserve must provide a complete environment for its occupants. There must be a sufficient variety of vegetation for the herbivorous animals and room for them to move around with the seasons as they normally do. There must also be enough carnivores to prevent the numbers of herbivores from getting out of hand.

Conservation does not mean that all the carnivores in the reserve must be destroyed. Apart from the fact that they must be conserved, too, they must play their natural part in maintaining the balance. Ideally, in a reserve, life should go on just as it did before man started to interfere. This is not always the case, for not all reserves provide a complete environment. In cases like this it may be necessary for man to step in and, by providing additional facilities or even by killing off some members of a species that has got out of hand, set things right again.

Game reserves can be a big tourist attraction, and in some African reserves herbivores such as antelopes have been shot as lion food by game wardens, who are careful to weed out the specimens which can be spared. Lions can thus be induced to feed in places where they can be seen.

41

ZOOGEOGRAPHICAL REGIONS

Palearctic ⎫
Nearctic ⎬ Holarctic
Neotropical
Ethiopian
Oriental
Australasian

THE CAT FAMILY

Animal Geography

So far as is known the earliest members of the cat family lived in the Palearctic region. From here representatives of the family easily reached the Nearctic region. Even today Asia is separated from Alaska by less than a hundred miles of sea, and often animals of the same species are found on either side of the gap. In the past, too, this gap was frequently above water. Other early cats reached the Ethiopian and Oriental regions. The Neotropical region was reached with more difficulty, as for much of the time South America

has been an island continent. The Australasian region proved too inaccessible. The cats, like most other highly developed mammals, never got there until they were taken there by man.

Once each region was colonized, the cats there, being more or less isolated from others of their kind, tended to diverge in appearance and habits, forming new species. However, it is possible for animals of the same species to colonize more than one region, as pumas do the Nearctic and Neotropical regions. Nevertheless, these *zoogeographical* regions provide an excellent basis for understanding the distribution of the cat species, as well as other land animals.

Classification

Carolus Linnaeus, a Swedish naturalist who lived from 1707 to 1778, originated the method by means of which living things are classified. His observation of plants and animals led him to see that sometimes two organisms of different kinds resemble each other quite closely in structure, while differing to a lesser or greater degree from others. He therefore proposed that animals of the same kind should be placed in the same *species,* and that this species should be in the same *genus* with other very similar species. Broadly similar *genera* (the plural of genus) were placed in the same *order,* orders were grouped in *classes,* and so on. The cats were part of the class Mammalia, and Linnaeus thought that all cats were so much alike that they could be put into a single genus, *Felis.*

The tenth edition of Linnaeus' book *Systema Naturae,* published in 1758, began the system which is still, with modifications, in use today. Animals are no longer classified purely on the basis of similarity of structure. The important factor nowadays is that animals within the same group must be related to each other, sharing the same ancestors. However, as related animals tend to look alike it very often comes to the same thing. To make the system more flexible some new groups have been introduced. Species are still placed in genera, but these are now sorted into *families*—a grouping not used by Linnaeus—which in their turn are placed in orders and classes.

Within the classification used today, the cats are thought to form a family, the Felidae, within the order Carnivora. Once the cats were placed in a single family it became possible to be fussier about the genus. Within Linnaeus' genus *Felis* there were obviously cats of several broad types, and zoologists began to sort these out, forming new genera in the process. At one time no fewer than twenty-three genera of cats were recognized. At this point there arose a feeling that the splitting process had gone too far—that not all of the named genera were really as distinct as their status made them out to be. A process of grouping them together again, so as to reduce their number, began. When this trend ground to a halt it was generally accepted by most authorities that the cat family in fact contained three genera.

The big cats, actually distinguished by the structure of their larynges rather than their size, formed the genus *Leo* (sometimes called *Panthera*). The small cats remained in the old genus *Felis*. The Cheetah, which is distinct in a number of ways—it cannot retract its claws, for example—is alone in the genus *Acinonyx*. Recently zoologists have tended to agree that the clouded leopard, intermediate between the big and small cats, belongs in the genus it once had before, *Neofelis*, and that the distinctive snow leopard should be *Uncia*.

At the present time there are thought to be thirty-six species of cats forming five genera.

Carolus Linnaeus originated the system of classifying living things in 1758. He placed all cats in a single group or *genus* called *Felis*. Nowadays, zoologists classify cats into five such groups.

CATS OF THE GENUS FELIS AND GENUS NEOFELIS

The Domestic Cat

It is difficult to be certain exactly when the association between the domestic cat and man began. Archaeologists have unearthed the bones of cats near remains left by early man, but the bones of wild and domestic cats are very similar, and the bones of wild animals are often found near the remains of human dwellings. Wild cats may not have made such good eating as some other game, but perhaps our ancestors could not afford to be fussy.

Even the identity of the wild species from which the domestic cat sprang is a matter for doubt. It is not unlike the European wild cat, but neither is it unlike some of the other wild cats of Africa and Asia, which are closely related. Wild cats of all these types may be descended from *Felïs lunensis,* which flourished in Europe just over a million years ago, and they all resemble each other closely in structure, differing mainly in the color and pattern of their fur.

The best guess is that the cat was first domesticated by the Egyptians some time before 1600 B.C. Perhaps African wild cats, *Felis libyca,* found that small rodents were common and easily caught near man's dwellings and eventually, emboldened by their success, even began to enter the houses, where they were tolerated as destroyers of vermin. Once the Egyptians had accepted the cat it rapidly rose in esteem, being regarded as sacred to the goddess Ubasti or Pasht. Her name, it is thought, has been associated with the cat ever since, although by now in the corrupted form— 'Puss'. Those who killed a cat in Egypt were severely punished, and when a cat died its owners went into mourning. Dead cats were mummified and buried with great reverence.

From Egypt, cats spread along the trade routes to Greece and Italy. This was a slow process, for Egyptians were reluctant to part with them. By the time of Christ, cats had become popular pets amongst the Romans. They were thus introduced to all parts of the Roman Empire. They have been popular ever since, although by the Middle Ages they had long since ceased being regarded as sacred in any way.

On the contrary, the cat was sometimes thought of as the familiar of witches. This idea has just lingered on into our own time, when some people think of cats as sinister, while others regard them as lucky, especially black cats.

Domestic cats usually weigh about seven pounds, although very fat specimens can weigh over twice as much. They are fully grown at about a year old and normally have a lifespan of up to twelve years, although exceptional individuals live to more than twenty. The females usually give birth to from four to six kittens and can breed two or three times a year. They are generally devoted mothers and the father takes no part in rearing the young.

Some domestic cats are self-supporting and are easily able to catch their own food.

The tabby is just one of the many varieties of domestic cats. Becoming domesticated must have entailed undergoing profound psychological changes, for all the wild cats of the present day are shy and retiring. Domestication was probably a gradual process that took several hundreds of years to complete.

Domestic Varieties

In the wild, members of the same species from the same part of the world usually resemble each other closely. The average animal is very well adapted for its life and if, during the normal course of breeding, young of a different color or shape should appear, then the chances are that these freaks will be less well adapted than the parents, and will have little chance of survival. 'Freaks' do occur in the wild, but are usually eliminated by natural selection. Sometimes, however, they provide the stock from which a new species or variety could evolve.

When man domesticates animals and controls their choice of mates, all this is changed. Human beings are fascinated by novelty. When freaks occur they are carefully reared and, if it is possible, bred to others that resemble them so as to produce more of their kind. In domesticated animals 'abnormal' shapes and colors become almost the rule rather than the exception.

As everyone knows, domestic cats come in a wide variety and mixture of colors—black, white, gray and ginger. The tabby pattern is the least changed, although even tabbies often show blotches rather than the stripes of wild cats.

The dark points of Siamese cats are the result of an ususual hereditary factor which determines the colors of their coats. On the warmer parts of the body this produces light-colored hairs, but on the cooler extremities it produces a darker coloring.

The length of the fur also varies in different breeds of domesticated cats; Persian Cats have long hair. There is some variation in body shape, too, although less than with some other domestic animals. Domestic dogs vary in size from the Chihuahua to the Great Dane and show an almost equally varied range of shapes. They almost form a living catalogue of the genetic disasters which can be thrown up by a stock of animals. The dwarf legs of the Dachshund and the stunted head of the Bulldog are examples. Domestic cats show less variety perhaps, partly because they are more difficult to keep in confinement. Breeders have therefore been unable to keep stocks pure for many generations, inbreeding until the line becomes 'pure' and the real oddities appear. Cats' heredity probably contains as much variation as that of dogs, but the variations that occur are not always readily apparent.

Domestic cats show great variety in fur and marking. The Siamese cat (*left*) has unusual dark points in its coat and startling blue eyes. The Persian cat (*right*) is well known for its beautiful long-haired coat.

The European Wild Cat

The English name of the European wild cat (*Felis silvestris*) is a little misleading, for the range of this species extends from Britain, through Europe, into western Asia, although it is now found only in out-of-the-way forested and mountainous areas.

At a quick glance it may not be easy to distinguish a wild cat from a domestic tabby which has run wild, as often happens. Besides this, there is always the possibility that a 'wild cat' which is reported is not pure-bred, but is the result of a misalliance between a domestic cat and a true wild cat, for the two species interbreed readily. However, wild cats have black stripes rather than the black blotches usually seen on domestic tabbies, and the black tip of their tails is rounded rather than pointed. It is reasonably easy to identify dead specimens, for wild cats have larger skulls and teeth than tame cats, although surprisingly their intestines are considerably shorter. Both wild and domestic cats are about the same size.

Wild cats usually hunt on their own, each animal keeping to an area of about 150 acres which is crossed by paths and punctuated by resting places and trees upon which the claws are regularly sharpened. This habit of sharpening the claws may also be a means of marking out the territory. Wild cats are most active when it is dry, and dawn and dusk are the most favored times for hunting.

They do not ignore small, tasty morsels like grasshoppers and beetles, but small mammals such as mice and voles make up the bulk of their food. They also hunt birds and sometimes tackle mammals the size of a small deer or a lamb. If they do, they usually content themselves with tearing off the head and eating the brains.

In the spring the males wander more widely than usual, calling noisily. Mating takes place, and after a gestation period of 63 days, the kittens are born in a den beneath the roots of a fallen tree or among rocks. This compares with an average of 58 days for the domestic cat. There are usually from two to four kittens, and their father plays no part in bringing them up. They leave their mother in the autumn and are fully grown at about a year. If they survive the first few dangerous months they may live for a number of years, for apart from man they have no enemies.

The European wild cat was once widely
distributed in Britain and Europe. It now
survives only in sparsely settled forested
areas of its former range.

The African Wild Cat

The African wild cat (*Felis libyca*) is obviously closely related to the Euopean Wild Cat, and some experts regard the two as different varieties of the same species. It has a wide range in Africa, being found in all areas apart from the great deserts and the equatorial forests. Like many other African mammals it is also found in Arabia (which forms part of the Ethiopian region), and from there its range extends to Syria and eastward to India. The cats that inhabit the Mediterranean islands of Sardinia and Corsica also belong to this species.

This cat is a little larger than the domestic cat, the average weight being about eight pounds, but African wild cats and domestic cats interbreed freely when the opportunity occurs. In appearance the African wild cat is not unlike its European cousin, but the stripes on the body are not so distinct, and the underside of the body sometimes has a yellowish tinge. The backs of the ears are always reddish yellow.

It is usually active at night, but it sometimes can be seen in daylight on cool, cloudy days. It prefers thinly forested country where it makes a den under the ground or among bushes. It hunts birds and small mammals.

The Sand Cat

The sand cat (*Relis margarita*) inhabits semidesert areas of North Africa (although its range does not extend into the Sahara Desert), Arabia and parts of the Middle East, ex-

The African wild cat resembles a long-legged large domestic tabby.

The sand cat hunts jerboas and other small mammals.

tending as far north as southern Russia. It is about the size of the domestic cat and is plain colored with few signs of stripes, except on the legs. The color varies from yellow-brown to gray-brown, but the backs of the ears always have a black patch, and there are three dark rings at the end of the tail, one extending to the tip. Like some other desert mammals, such as the desert foxes, it has large ears which are widely spaced and situated rather toward the sides of the head. Although seldom seen, this species is easily identified by its footprints, as the pads of the feet are almost covered by hair.

In southern Russia, sand cats hide during the day among bushes, where they dig shallow burrows in the sand between the roots. They hunt ground squirrels, hares, sand voles and jerboas. The young, about four in number, are born in April.

The Jungle Cat

The jungle cat (*Felis chaus*) is rather larger than the cats so far considered, and may weigh up to twenty pounds. It occurs in Egypt, the Middle East and Asia Minor, Russia just east of the Caspian Sea, India, Ceylon, Nepal, Burma, the Indo-Chinese region and Thailand. It is gray-brown with faintly striped markings, except for the tail, which has prominent black rings. The underside is white. The short tail and the presence of small tufts on the ears suggest that this species may have some affinity with the lynxes.

The jungle cat usually keeps to thick bushes and almost impenetrable reeds, often in low-lying, swampy forests, but if these are not available, cornfields or tall grass seem to suit it just as well. Although it is most often active at night, it is not exclusively nocturnal and is quite often about in the daytime. It climbs well and, although it sometimes hunts mammals such as hares, birds are its main quarry. It kills water-fowl, pheasants, francolins, partridges and even—in India—peacocks. If human dwellings are nearby, it boldly raids poultry runs.

In Russia the jungle cat's mating season is in February or March, and at this time the voice of the male, not unlike that

The jungle cat inhabits dense cover in the Middle East and Asia.

54

of the domestic cat but deeper and louder, is often raised in amorous dispute. The females have between three and five kittens in April or May in a dry den under the ground. Often the unused home of a badger, fox or a porcupine is pressed into service. The entrance to the den is usually well camouflaged.

The Chinese Desert Cat

The Chinese desert cat (*Felis bieti*) was first discovered only toward the end of the nineteenth century, and very little is known about it even today. It is about the same size as the domestic cat and appears to inhabit dry grasslands—perhaps semideserts would be a better description—in Mongolia and the Chinese provinces of Kansu and Szechuan.

Like many mammals from dry areas, it is rather light in color, the back being grayish-yellow, the flanks a little darker, and the underside lighter. The rear part of the body and the face are lightly marked with broken bars. The tail has several dark rings and a black tip. The light coloring of desert animals serves as camouflage and may also assist in reflecting the sun's heat, rather than absorbing it as a dark coat would.

The Chinese desert cat is a little known cat inhabiting semidesert regions of the Far East.

The Leopard Cat

Small spotted cats are found in most tropical countries. It is unlikely that they all evolved from a single ancestor; their coats, which are light in color with rows of dark spots, have developed similarly to protect the animals in their various habitats. These habitats vary from forests and light jungle to open woodlands and grassy plains, but these cats are all much alike in appearance and habits. One of the most common is the leopard cat (*Felix bengalensis*). This cat is the most common wild cat of southeast Asia, where it is found in Burma, the Malay Peninsula, Sumatra, Java, Borneo and some of the Philippines. Its range also extends to northern India, Tibet, China and eastern Siberia. It is about as large as the domestic cat, and being heavily spotted, it has a superficial resemblance to a very small leopard. However; the spots are not grouped into rosettes as are those of the leopard. The color and spotting of the leopard cat are very variable, as is often the case with a species which has a wide range. A typical specimen from Sumatra has fewer markings than those from the mainland of Asia, while

The leopard cat is the commonest wild cat of southeast Asia.

Javan specimens have brighter, orange-brown fur, and those from Bali are duller. Individuals from the Philippine Islands are altogether smaller.

The leopard cat lives in hilly areas and secondary jungle, avoiding the thickest forest, and climbs actively. Its prey usually consists of large birds and small mammals up to the size of squirrels and hares, but it may occasionally kill a small deer. In India the young are born in May. There are usually three or four of them, and they are nursed in a den inside a cave or under fallen rocks.

The Rusty-Spotted Cat

The rusty-spotted cat (*Felis rubiginosa*) replaces its slightly larger relative, the leopard cat, in southern India and Ceylon. It is rust-colored with lines of brown blotches along its body. This cat frequents long grass and brushwood, sometimes hiding in the undergrowth around ditches in the middle of open country. It never penetrates thick jungle. The young, if taken early enough, can be tamed more easily than those of some other wild cats.

The rusty-spotted cat is found only in southern India and Ceylon.

The Flat-Headed Cat

The flat-headed cat (*Felis planiceps*) is one of the smallest of the family, weighing about 4½ pounds. It inhabits the Malay Peninsula, Borneo and Sumatra, but is nowhere common, or if it is, the fact has never been reported, for it is nocturnal in habit and could easily escape observation. The color of the fur is more or less uniformly brown, darker on the back and shading to white underneath. Many of the guard-hairs are white-tipped, and this gives the body a silver-gray appearance.

In relation to the size of the body, the legs are shorter than those of any other cat of the Oriental region. The tail is rather short too, being only about a third of the length of the head and body combined.

In Borneo it stays close to the banks of rivers; fish and frogs form an important part of its diet, but it also occasionally eats birds.

The Bay Cat

The bay cat (*Felis badius*) has a very restricted distribution, coming only from the island of Borneo. That little is known of its habits is not surprising, for until relatively recent years zoologists concentrated on dissecting dead animals, collecting their skins and bones, and classifying them. The study of animals in the field, especially rare and furtive ones from remote parts of the world, is very difficult, and many animals, including the bay cat, have never been the objects of such a study.

For information about their habits we have to rely on the anecdotes of hunters and casual observers, and even those are scanty.

The bay cat has fewer traces of dark spots or stripes than any other cat of the East Indies, although there may occasionally be faint stripes on the face. The back of the ears is black with a white spot, and there is another patch of this color on the underside of the tail tip. Not for the first time, it will be noticed, the pattern is most marked on those parts of the body which function as signals between members of the same species. The fur of the body is yellowish-brown, often with a red tinge. The bay cat is a little larger than the domestic cat.

The flat-headed cat from the Malay Peninsula,
Borneo and Sumatra is a relatively rare species.

The rare bay cat
lives only on Borneo.

The black-footed cat is a wild cat of
southern Africa. It is named after the
black fur on the underside of its feet.

The Black-Footed Cat

The black-footed cat (*Felis nigripes*) is an African species
with a range which includes the Kalahari Desert and other
parts of southern Africa. It is not a common species anywhere in this area. This is yet another species which has
been known to crossbreed with the domestic cat, although
the black-footed cat is slightly smaller in size.

This cat is pale tawny-brown, shading to white underneath and on the insides of the limbs. This very common
type of coloring is useful as camouflage. The colors cancel
out the effects of shadows when light falls from overhead,
thus making the animal appear not rounded, but flat and
insubstantial. On the neck and shoulders there are darker
lines, and the body is spotted.

The Caracal Lynx

The caracal lynx (*Felis caracal*) has the tufted ears and short tail typical of the lynxes and to some extent replaces the larger northern lynx in warmer parts of the Old World. Its range extends from the deserts of southern Russia to northern India, the Middle East, Arabia and many parts of Africa. It is found in dry regions from the desolate and wind-swept plateaus of Asia to the mountainous semideserts of Africa, whether they are open or densely covered with bush. It is lightly built with a short 8-inch tail. The head and body together usually measure just over two feet long.

It is agile, and speedy over short distances and puts this ability to good use in hunting. Bursting from cover it hurls itself toward the prey. If this prey is a bird which attempts to fly away, it can leap into the air, grabbing it with its forelimbs. In Asia its prey consists of doves, hares, pikas (small mammals related to rabbits) and ground squirrels, while in Africa it is known to kill small antelopes and birds of all kinds. It may even attack eagles if it can surprise them when they are roosting at night.

The female usually has two or three young in an underground den or a hollow tree.

The caracal lynx has exceptionally long ears, ending in long tufts of hair.

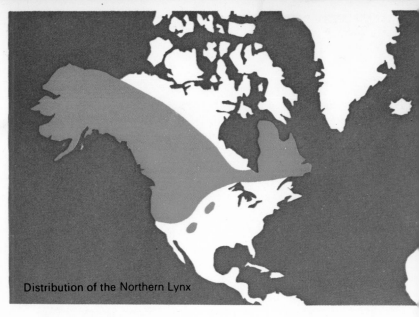

Distribution of the Northern Lynx

The Northern Lynx

The northern lynx (*Felis lynx*) has a range which originally included all the temperate forests of the Northern Hemisphere. The advance of civilization has resulted in the disappearance of the lynx from many of its former haunts, but in Europe they still exist in Spain and Portugal (where they are, however, in great danger of extinction), parts of Scandinavia, Poland, parts of the Balkans and Sardinia. Slightly different types of northern lynx exist, but all are regarded as a single species.

The lynx is a powerfully built cat with very sturdy limbs. Its tail is only about 4 inches long. Over short distances it can move very fast, although it lacks staying power and quickly tires. At lower speeds, it can cover long distances. It is an expert climber, jumping from one tree to another with ease and often hiding among the branches.

The lynx is cautious and cunning and moves quietly. Its high-pitched soft voice is seldom raised. In remote areas it is quite often active by day, but in the vicinity of man it becomes more wary, hunting mainly by night. Animals the size of roe deer and grouse, or in America snowshoe hares, are the normal prey. Unlike many cats it will never eat carrion, and despite its size and power this lynx rarely attacks man.

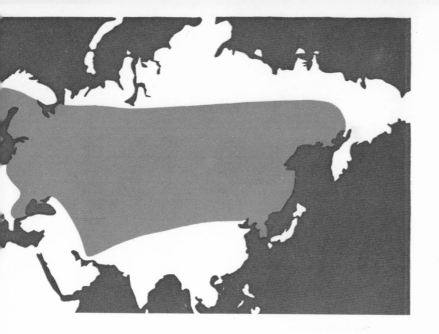

The northern lynx lives in dense forest or in thick bush on mountain sides.

The bobcat lives in North America and Mexico.

The Bobcat

The bobcat (*Felis rufa*) is closely related to the lynx. Its range extends from southern Canada to southern Mexico. A full-grown male bobcat may weigh eighteen pounds and is smaller than a lynx. The two species therefore illustrate Bergman's Rule, which states that animals from warm climates are in general smaller than related animals from cooler regions.

The bobcat inhabits more open country than the lynx, preferring scrub, thickets and undulating ground. Hunting mainly at night, it preys on rodents such as mice, wood rats, chipmunks, pocket gophers and squirrels, as well as rabbits and birds. Occasionally it goes after bigger game, hunting white-tailed deer or birds the size of a turkey.

The majority of bobcat litters are born in the spring. The gestation period is about fifty days and two or three young are the usual number. Youngsters born in the spring can fend for themselves by the time their first winter arrives, but they may stay with their mother until they are a year old.

Pallas's Cat

The Pallas cat (*Felis manul*) owes its name to Pallas, the man who discovered the species in 1778, rather than the goddess Pallas Athene. It was first found among stony, steppe-like country, although it also inhabits woods from east of the Caspian Sea to Persia, Tibet, Mongolia and western China. Possibly this is the species which replaces the European wild cat, living very much the same life as its relative but in these different regions.

The basic coat color is orange-brown, but the white and black rings around the eyes, the gray forehead with black spots and the white chin make this one of the most handsome of the small cats in appearance. The small, rounded ears are set well toward the sides of head and are yellowish-gray, and the hair on the sides of the face is long.

It hunts partridges, pikas and small rodents such as voles and mice.

Pallas's cat lives in central Asia.

65

The serval (*left*) inhabits bush country in Africa. It prefers areas where the bush is not too thick, and although it is occasionally seen at the edges of forests, it is never found in very dry regions or very far from water. The marbled cat (*opposite*) of Asia is seldom seen, partly because it is shy and nocturnal, but also because it is rather rare and inhabits forests, where cover is plentiful. Its fur is very long, and the markings vary a great deal from one individual to another.

The Serval

The serval (*Felis serval*) is a slenderly built, medium-sized cat which weighs about 34 pounds. It has rather a small head surmounted by very large ears, long slender legs and a short tail only about a foot in length. It is an inhabitant of bush country and is found over a wide area of Africa south of the Sahara Desert.

Although the ears are not tufted, this cat shows some resemblance to the lynxes and, like the caracal, it sometimes slinks toward its prey and then, breaking cover, sprints over the last few yards. In this way it often captures medium-sized birds, such as guinea-fowl, and mammals, including hares and duikers. Good eyesight is vital to the success of this method of hunting, and it is hardly surprising that the serval is often seen hunting by day. It also eats rodents, sometimes digging them from their burrows.

After a gestation period of about seventy days the female usually has three young, either in a nest among the dense, dry grass, or in a den underground. Often the discarded burrow of an aardvark is used for this purpose.

The Marbled Cat

The marbled cat (*Felis marmorata*) is very similar to the clouded leopard in appearance, but is smaller, being only a little larger than the domestic cat. Its range extends from Nepal and the slopes of the Himalayas, through Burma and the Malay Peninsula, to Sumatra and Borneo. It is a rare animal.

This cat is said to hunt on the ground in clearings and along river banks, but in view of its resemblance to the clouded leopard, which often climbs, this is by no means certain. It may well be that the marbled cat is less likely to attract attention when it hunts aloft, where its lighter weight would be supported by even more slender branches than those used by the clouded leopard. A long tail is an asset to a climber, being a useful means of adjusting weight distribution and therefore assisting balance.

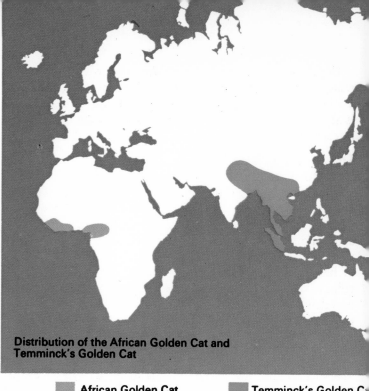

Distribution of the African Golden Cat and Temminck's Golden Cat

African Golden Cat   Temminck's Golden C

Temminck's Golden Cat

Temminck's golden cat (*Felis temmincki*), which comes from Tibet, southwest China, northern India, Burma, the Indo-Chinese region, Thailand, Malaya and Sumatra, is often confused with the African golden cat. Not only do the two species look very much alike, but the true facts are even more confusing than is usually realized. The African golden cat was first described and named by Temminck, a famous naturalist of the early 1800's who was the author of a monograph on the cats. The other species of golden cat had not then been discovered. Later, in 1827, a member of the Asiatic species turned up as one of the very first inhabitants of Regent's Park Zoo. It was named by two Fellows of the Zoological Society and, in naming it, they decided to honor Temminck. Temminck's golden cat is accordingly the species which Temminck did not discover.

Both species of golden cats are probably very closely related, and this explains their great similarity of appearance. Temminck's golden cat is slightly the larger of the two. It is also a rare animal, but it is said to live among rocks in tall forests.

The African Golden Cat

The African golden cat *(Felis aurata)* is a handsome and rare species from western Africa where it inhabits high, deciduous forests near the coast from Sierra Leone to the north of the Congo. It owes its name to the golden-brown color of the short and very lustrous fur. Some members of this species are much more gray in coloring, and this is not entirely a matter of heredity, for one zoo specimen once changed from one color to the other. The back is usually a slightly darker shade, and darker spots are visible from the flanks downward. The tail bears no spots or stripes, and the backs of the ears are almost black. The head and body combined are about 28 inches long, and the tail is 16 inches.

The African golden cat much resembles Temminck's golden cat of southern Asia.

The fishing cat lives in marshy land in southern Asia and is believed to hunt fish as well as small mammals.

The Fishing Cat

The fishing cat *(Felis viverrina)* is heavily built and rather short-legged. Although the head and body together are about 32 inches long, the tail measures only about a foot. An average specimen weighs about 17 pounds.

Its Bengali name was 'Mach-bagral' and to this it owes its English name, which is an accurate translation. However, there is some doubt as to whether the species is as fond of fish as the name suggests. Some experts say that it has never been seen catching or eating fish, but others believe that it does do so occasionally by scooping them out of the water with its paws.

It is usually found near water, for it inhabits low-lying, swampy forests in Ceylon, India, former Indo-China, Thailand, Malaya, Java and Sumatra. It is quite common in some places. Its spotted mouse-gray or tawny-gray coat is one of the most harsh in texture to be found in the cat family and, to give support to the theory that it really does fish, the toes are very slightly webbed. It is certainly a bold and intrepid hunter and has been known to attack goats. It has even been said to carry off human babies.

The Ocelot

The ocelot *(Felis pardalis)* is nocturnal in areas where it is frequently disturbed by man, but otherwise it hunts both by day and by night. It lives in forests and thick vegetation where the stripes and spots of its fur blend well with the leafy shadows, providing excellent camouflage. It occurs rarely in the southern United States, but is common in Central and South America, being found as far south as Paraguay.

A large male may weigh as much as 34 pounds and measure 4½ feet overall, one third of this being the tail. Because of the handsome markings of the coat, the fur has commercial value. These markings vary a great deal from one habitat to another, lighter forms being found in more open country.

Being a good climber it often spends the day asleep amongst the branches of a tree, but much of its hunting is done on the ground. It eats opossums, small and medium-sized rodents up to the size of the agouti (a favorite prey), peccaries and small deer. It rarely eats birds, but tackles reptiles including fairly large lizards. One ocelot is reported to have killed a boa seven feet in length.

The ocelot is known for its beautiful marked fur, which has commercial value.

The Margay

The margay *(Felis wiedii)* or Wied's tiger cat is a close relation of the ocelot and has very much the same distribution,
being rare in the southern parts of the United States but
more common in the forests of Central and South America.
It extends as far south as Paraguay and Argentina. The head
and body of an average specimen are just under two feet in
length, and the tail adds just over another foot to this.

The soft fur is yellow-brown, being darker on the back of
the body and grayer on the head. The top of the head and
the cheeks are deeper yellow in tone. Between the cheeks
and the eyes there are conspicuous white markings. The
whole animal is marked with prominent black lines and
spots. Toward the tip of the tail the spots join together to
form complete rings.

Little is known of the habits of the margay in the wild.
Perhaps, being smaller than the ocelot, it spends more of its
time in trees hunting birds. The fact that the tail of the margay is relatively longer than that of the ocelot lends some
support to this view.

The Tiger Cat

The tiger cat *(Felis tigrina)* is sometimes also known as the
American tiger cat to distinguish it from the African tiger cat,
another name for the African golden cat. A species of animal
may have a number of common names, but names of this
kind have no scientific value. Scientific names are another
matter and are subject to strict rules. A species is only allowed
to have one scientific name. By definition a species is an
interbreeding population of organisms distinguishable from
other such populations with which there is no interbreeding.
In practice, however, criteria for this definition are hard to
establish, and as new facts are gathered, species classification changes. The range of the tiger cat overlaps that of the
margay and the ocelot, and it is often difficult to know which
species is referred to in accounts of spotted, forest-dwelling
South American cats. Also such accounts are scanty for, zoo-
logically speaking, South America is the least well known of
the continents.

The tiger cat inhabits forests and woodlands from Costa
Rica in Central America to northern South America. It is
a good climber and hunts birds and small mammals.

The margay (*top*) resembles the ocelot in appearance. It is usually smaller in size, although an exceptional animal may be almost as big as an ocelot. The tiger cat (*below*) is also known as the American tiger cat and as the little spotted cat. Both cats inhabit South and Central America, and margays are occasionally found in the southern United States.

The Mountain Cat

The mountain cat *(Felis jacobita)* is sometimes also known as the Andean cat. This is yet another species which is only found in South America. The various cats of this continent are all descended from North American ancestors but have evolved into very distinctive species.

The mountain cat lives in the mountains of Chile, Peru, Bolivia and Argentina. As it comes from the cooler heights where a bright orange-brown coat would be conspicuous, the fur is a brownish-gray with darker markings on its sides and rings on its tail. The head and body together are about 30 inches long and the tail about 18 inches. It hunts small and medium-sized rodents, including the wild relations of the guinea pig.

The mountain cat is one of the many unusual cats of South America. For most of its history, the Neotropical Region has been completely cut off from other regions by the sea, although land bridges such as the Isthmus of Panama have periodically risen above the waves. Because of this long isolation, the cats only reached South America from North America some two million years ago.

Geoffroy's cat hunts birds and small mammals, often plunging from low branches onto its prey.

Geoffroy's Cat

Geoffroy's cat *(Felis geoffroyi)* is named after Geoffroy Saint-Hilaire, a French naturalist who lived in the nineteenth century. The range of this species extends from Bolivia in the north to Patagonia, southern Argentina.

Like the mountain cat, Geoffroy's cat is usually found in cool and steeply sloping upland areas, but Geoffroy's cat is perhaps more often an inhabitant of the foothills than the mountains themselves. Being an excellent climber, Geoffroy's cat does not venture too far from trees and is not found above the tree line.

75

The Jaguarundi

The jaguarundi *(Felis yagouaroundi)* has a maximum length of four feet, and 18 inches of this consists of the tail. This is perhaps the most surprising in appearance of all the cats. Most of the family bear a strong likeness to each other, whatever the differences in size and markings may be, but the jaguarundi in some ways resembles an otter, or at least some other member of the weasel family, rather than a cat. Its body is graceful, but rather long and sinuous, and this effect is increased by the shortness of the legs. Despite its length the jaguarundi is a lightweight animal, weighing twenty pounds.

Gray and brown jaguarundis (*below*) belong to the same species.

For a cat it has rather small ears and an unusual snub nose. The fur is uniform in color, but there are two different color varieties. At one time it was thought that the reddish-brown individuals, known as *eyras,* belonged to a different species from the grayer jaguarundis, but we now know that they all belong to the same species and that the different colored varieties are not found in different parts of the animal's range. Normally the coloring of a wild animal is related to its mode of life, being adapted for survival. The reason for these different color phases in some species of the cat family is unknown.

At all events the jaguarundi is obviously a highly individual species of cat, different in every way from the animal with which its name might be confused, the much larger, heavily spotted jaguar.

The jaguarundi is found from the Argentine and Paraguay in South America to southern Texas in the United States. It is often spoken of as a forest-dwelling species, which is scarcely what would be expected of a plain-colored animal, but it also seems to frequent open glades and clearings on the forest fringe. It is found in bush country and is also abundant in the open on some savannahs.

This cat is equally active by day and at night and is an excellent climber, often traveling large distances through a forest entirely by way of the branches, although it can also move with considerable speed on the ground. The suppleness of the body adequately compensates for the deficiencies of the legs when running to an even greater extent than in other members of the cat family.

Jaguarundis hunt on their own, catching ground-living birds such as tinamous and trumpeters, small mammals and perhaps some frogs and fish. One very reliable observer has reported seeing them climbing high up in fig trees and feeding on wild figs in the company of howler monkeys. If this is true it is the most surprising thing of all about these unconventional cats. As a family, the cats are the most purely carnivorous of mammals and do not normally eat fruit.

The female usually has two or three young after a gestation period of up to 70 days. The young are slightly spotted at birth and, as is frequently the case in the cat family, the father plays no part in rearing them.

The kodkod inhabits woodlands in the foothills of the Andes in Chile.

The Kodkod

The kodkod *(Felis guigna)* lives in the foothills of the Andes in Chile. Although this is still part of the Neotropical region, it is effectively cut off by the long mountain chain so it is not surprising that in such isolation yet another South American species of cat should have evolved.

The kodkod is quite small, the head and body together being about 18 inches long and the tail another nine inches. The gray-brown fur is handsomely marked with rows of darker spots, and the tail is encircled with black rings.

This species normally inhabits woodlands, hunting small mammals such as rodents, but has been known to raid domestic poultry runs. The raiders were said to have come in parties. If this is true, mothers and their growing families may have been involved, or alternatively this species may be more social when hunting than any other species of cat, except for the lion.

The Pampas Cat

The pampas cat *(Felis colocolo)* is another species about which very little is known. It is to be hoped that more will be learned of it before it is too late, as the pampas cat is in some danger of becoming extinct. But little time may remain, for this species like so many others cannot cope with the disturbance caused by human civilization and is much less common now than it was a hundred years ago. It was then widespread in Argentina and Uruguay, occurring not only in grasslands, as its English name suggests, but also amongst reeds in swampier conditions.

It is about as large as a domestic cat and has a relatively long tail. The fur is gray, becoming lighter under the body, and it has brown markings on the body. Along the back is a distinct crest of longer hair. Hunting is said to take place mainly at night, and the prey consists of small birds and mammals. There are normally from one to three kittens in a litter.

The pampas cat is one of the rarest of the wild cats.

The Puma — appearance and distribution

The puma *(Felis concolor)* is considerably larger than other members of the genus *Felis,* but is nevertheless a true member of the genus. Like the smaller cats it purrs both as it breathes in and as it breathes out — a feature which is a direct result of the structure of the larynx (or Adam's apple) and typical of the genus. The cry is also a typical, throaty, high-pitched

'yowl' rather than the roar of the big cats of the genus *Leo.* The puma's affinities show in other ways, too. In proportion it is more like the smaller cats, the head being relatively small in comparison with the body. In feeding, the puma, like the domestic cat, makes little use of the forepaws, which are placed firmly on the ground as the animal squats over its food. In contrast to this the big cats usually rest on their elbows, holding the food with their paws. In every way then, the puma is most like the smaller cats rather than the larger ones in spite of its size.

Many species of animals have more than one common name, but few have so many as the puma. In the United States alone its names include 'cougar', 'mountain lion', 'catamount' and 'painter', but its range extends far more widely than this and covers as wide a range of climates as that of any other kind of mammal. Formerly it was widespread in North America, but with the advent of civilization its range has been reduced. It now occurs in the Rocky Mountains extending as far north as western Canada. In the south its range includes plains and forests as well as deserts, and it extends through

The puma usually has a litter of two or three kittens, but up to six may be born.

Central America and South America to Patagonia, though it is not common in equatorial forests.

Not surprisingly, with a range like this, the puma is a very variable species. Individuals from populations in cooler climates are, on the average, larger than those from the tropics. This is another example of Bergman's Rule in action. The males are usually bigger than the females, and the head and body of a large male would measure about five feet with the tail another three feet long. The weight of an animal this size could be 260 pounds. A small male, on the other hand, might weigh only 80 pounds. Pumas vary in color from light brown to, in a few cases, black. Little wonder that some people who have studied them think that more than one species is involved. Even so most experts think that the puma is a single species, although one zoologist held the extreme view that there were at least a hundred different species of puma.

The Puma—behavior

Being one of the larger carnivores of the Americas, the puma naturally concentrates on hunting fairly large prey. On the whole its range coincides quite closely with the range of deer of such species as the white-tailed deer and the mule deer, and there can be little doubt that these provide the chief prey. In the United States it has been found that, on the average, the puma kills one deer each week, although the record seems to be held by a bloodthirsty and successful individual which killed a total of seven deer in ten days. Having made a kill and eaten its fill, the puma hides the carcass, often dragging it for some distance and covering it with sticks and leaves. Having done this, it may come back to feed again later. One such kill is known to have been revisited ten times.

Other animals killed by pumas include peccaries, pacas, agoutis, spiny rats, iguanas and, in Patagonia, young sea-lions. In Peru they hunt vicunas, which are fleet-footed relatives of the camels. Pumas have been known to tackle even animals as large as horses, but they rarely attack man. Bear-

ing in mind that they are such large animals and often hunt in the open, pumas are seen relatively rarely. This is because they are cautious and shy and are most often active at night.

Although they keep to a more or less fixed territory, they are great wanderers within this beat which may extend for over a hundred miles. Having made a kill the puma may lie up in the same district for a few days, but it soon moves on to another area.

After a gestation period of about 14 weeks the female Puma gives birth to a litter of usually two or three kittens, although exceptionally there may be as many as six. At first the kittens' coats bear prominent dark spots and the tail is ringed, but these are lost later, although the dark spots on either side of the muzzle remain throughout life, and dark hairs also remain at the tip of the tail. The kittens soon become very active and playful and are weaned at ten weeks old, although it takes two years for them to become fully grown. Although they grow up more slowly than domestic cats, pumas live no longer than the tame species, and few of them reach an age of fifteen years.

White-tailed deer are the usual prey of the puma. On the average a puma kills one deer every week. Pumas will attack mammals as large as horses, but they rarely go for human beings.

The Clouded Leopard

The clouded leopard *(Neofelis nebulosa)* is in some ways intermediate between the larger cats *(Leo)* and the smaller cats *(Felis)*, and for this reason some experts feel it best to place the animal in a genus of its own, *Neofelis*.

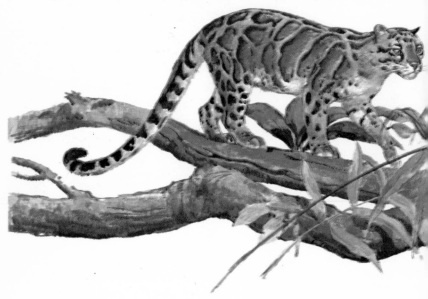

The species has an Oriental distribution, being found in Nepal and northern India, Burma, former Indo-China, southern China (including the islands of Hainan and Formosa), Thailand, Malaya, Sumatra and Borneo. Ever since being discovered in 1821 these animals seem to have been rather rare, or at least to have been seen rarely. Perhaps they are not uncommon in certain places, but of all the cats of Asia, clouded leopards are found in the thickest jungles. As they are great climbers and spend most of their time concealed in the leafy seclusion of the branches, they must often remain unseen.

The head and the body of the clouded leopard are three feet or more in length. The long tail, which is a useful adaptation to a climbing life, adds another 30 inches, but despite its length the clouded leopard is not very heavy. It has rather

The clouded leopard
is a great climber,
spending most of its
time in trees.

short limbs and a graceful slender body, and the only recorded weight—44½ pounds for an adult male—is surprisingly light. Of course, in trees weight can be a disadvantage, for lighter animals can venture along thinner branches. Among the shadows the beautiful blotches of the coat with their less intense, 'clouded' centers, provide excellent camouflage. In elderly specimens—and clouded leopards in zoos have lived to be sixteen years old—all of the coloring in the center of the blotches tends to disappear leaving only the broken, black margins.

Clouded leopards hunt mainly at night and are presumed to prey on birds and small mammals, although they have been known to attack domestic sheep, pigs, goats and dogs. Nothing is known of their breeding habits in the wild, but in zoos litters of from one to four cubs have been born.

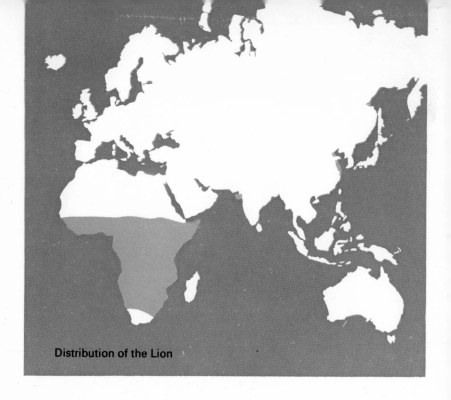

Distribution of the Lion

THE BIG CATS (GENUS LEO)

The Lion—distribution and appearance

In prehistoric times and even slightly later, the lion (*Leo leo*) had a continuous range, which included southeast Europe, the Middle East and India, as well as Africa. Inevitably the interests of such a large and predatory animal clashed with those of man, who wished to preserve his flocks and herds of domestic animals, and the lion, despite its power, was no match for the cunning of his human adversary. Lions have now dispersed from much of their former range, and, in the process, their distribution has become divided up into separate pockets.

The European lions were first to go and then those of Asia started to disappear. Today it is just possible that a few remain in Persia, but the only lions that certainly remain on the Asian continent are those that inhabit the Gir Forest near the northwest coast of India. At the last count there

Lioness

Lion

were 285 of them in an area of 483 square miles, and they were holding their own, preying mainly on domestic cattle. About a hundred of these Asiatic lions are killed by man annually, but such is their birth rate that their numbers remain roughly constant.

By the beginning of the twentieth century the lions of North Africa had gone too. At the other end of the continent, those of southernmost Africa came under human pressure and disappeared. Most of the world's remaining lion population is, accordingly, in Africa south of the Sahara. In western Africa, lions occur as far west as Liberia, but most of the species live in eastern Africa where some of the large herds of ungulates upon which they depend for food still remain.

In appearance lions are a very variable species. As is well known, males have a mane of long hair on the head, shoulders, chest and elbows, and this is an especially variable feature. Some manes are a light, tawny brown and others are black, and the distribution of the hair shows equal variation.

A lioness usually has two or three cubs in a litter, but up to six may be born.

Perhaps several subspecies of lions do exist, but if so they can only be identified after examining a whole series of individuals and finding out the average typical of any particular area. For example, compared with African lions, most lions of Asia have a scantier mane on the head, but more profuse tufts on the elbows, chest and tail, whereas the coat itself grows rather more thickly, In size there is little difference between the lions of Asia and those of Africa.

The Lion—size and breeding

The average male is just under nine feet long overall, and ten feet is quite exceptional. An average weight would be 350 to 400 pounds, although higher figures have been recorded. Lionesses are usually smaller—perhaps eight feet long and with an average weight of 300 pounds. Of course individual variation occurs, and there is some overlap between the measurements of a small Lion and a large lioness.

Perhaps because of their greater size lions mature more slowly than do lionesses, which are sufficiently well developed to bear their first litter when they are between three and four years old. Although they may in some parts of their range show a tendency to breed mainly at a certain season, lions can breed at any time of the year. The most likely mate for a lioness will always be the largest, fiercest and most mature lion in the pride of which she forms part, but sometimes several adult males gather and clash for her favors. At such a time serious fights may occur.

After a gestation period of about 108 days, the cubs are born. There are usually two or three of them, but there may be as many as six. Their nursery will be among bushes in order to provide some degree of security, for although the cubs are born with their eyes partly open, they cannot see well until they are at least a week old and are at first helpless. Their fur is prominently marked with clusters of spots, especially on the head, which fade gradually. Indeed traces of spots can usually be found on the underside and the hind legs of even a mature animal.

The cubs are gradually weaned at about eight weeks. As they gain in strength they play vigorously, but they are not capable of killing their own prey until they are about two years old. Until this time they are dependent upon their mother and other members of the pride.

Lion cubs are playful creatures, remaining dependent on their mothers and the others of the pride until they are two years old.

The Lion—lifespan and hunting

A lion comes into its prime at four to five years old and is past its prime at the age of ten. We have little knowledge of the lifespan of wild lions. Undoubtedly, lions have a high death rate during their first year or so, and if they survive this period they will still be unlikely to reach old age. Wild animals rarely do, for life in the wild is hard and death from starvation, disease or the results of an accident is common. Zoo lions, which lead sheltered lives, may reach old age. One specimen in the Dublin Zoo lived to be twenty-five.

Lions hunt a wide variety of prey. They have been known

The tawny-brown coat of the lion acts as camouflage among the open grasslands, where it preys on herbivores such as antelopes.

to kill animals as small as rats and mice, and they are very fond of domestic chickens. They certainly feed on carrion, especially when game is scarce. Nevertheless, they are primarily adapted as hunters of large herbivores such as antelopes and zebra.

Lions often hunt by day, especially if they are undisturbed by man. Sometimes they work on their own, stalking their prey as any other cat would and then seeking to surprise it by covering the last few yards in a few bounds, reaching speeds of up to thirty miles an hour in the process. Alternatively, lying in ambush by a waterhole may sometimes yield results. Methods like these are of most value when the prey is isolated and not a member of a large herd, as is often the case with those large herbivores that still survive in western Africa.

Other methods are needed to kill an individual from a large mixed herd of gnu and zebra such as is found in eastern Africa. Sometimes the males, being the more conspicuous animals, act as beaters, trying to drive the prey towards the smaller but just as deadly females, who lurk in hiding. Under these conditions it is the lionesses who are most likely to make the actual kill. However, once the prey is frightened and on the move anything can happen, and the males often get their chance.

The Lion—making a kill and feeding

Lions use both their teeth and claws when making a kill, but their weight can also play a part. Sometimes the prey is bowled over by something like a flying football tackle before being dispatched. A single blow from a lion's massive paw can easily bowl over a medium-sized antelope. Larger prey is rarely attacked from the front, for lions are not invulnerable and have a healthy respect for butting heads and jabbing horns. In cases like this, they prefer to attack from the rear, clawing at the legs and thus disabling their prey before making their kill.

Once the kill has been made, the members of the pride lick up any blood which may have been shed and then disembowel their victim. The entrails are pulled out and put to the side and then the choicer morsels are eaten first.

Lions prefer kidneys and liver and then eat the thigh muscles, followed by the ribs. The tougher parts of the head, neck and back are left until later. Naturally not all members of the pride are equal in status, and high ranking animals feed first and get what might, in other circumstances, be called the lion's share.

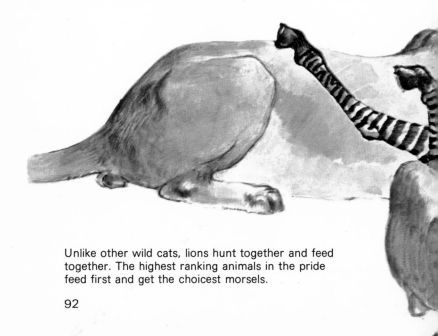

Unlike other wild cats, lions hunt together and feed together. The highest ranking animals in the pride feed first and get the choicest morsels.

If times are good and game is plentiful the pride may well be unable to eat all the food that is available. If this is so they may return later for another meal, although if the kill is in the open they will find little left, for such scavengers as the vultures, jackals and hyenas will have made the most of their opportunity.

Exactly how often wild lions kill and feed has been the subject of much discussion and little agreement. Probably it varies a great deal, according to the circumstances. However, it is certain that once the opportunity arises, a lion makes a huge meal and may consume forty or even sixty pounds of meat at a sitting. Meat is a very filling food and requires thorough digestion, particularly as it is swallowed in large chunks. A single large meal may therefore be enough to satisfy a lion's appetite for up to a week. On this basis one kill every six or seven days would suffice to keep a small pride well fed.

Zoo lions feed more often than wild ones do but get smaller meals and so eat about the same total amount of meat. A meal of ten or twelve pounds of meat a day for six days, followed by a day's fast, is the rule in the lion houses of many zoos.

Lion Behavior

Lions have little to occupy themselves with between meals. By nature they are lazy animals and are content to spend much of their time resting. It is rare for adult animals to indulge in exercise for its own sake, and in the few cases where it is reported, it may well be that what has been seen has been misinterpreted. As has already been pointed out, every feature of a wild animal is adapted and geared to the need to survive. Unnecessary expenditure of energy would be inefficient and lower an animal's capacity for survival, and it is therefore unlikely to occur. Lions get enough exercise when hunting or when forced to move to another hunting ground because game is scarce or because they have been disturbed.

Although the lion has few natural enemies other than man, it has rival hunters to contend with. The presence of human competition in the form of big-game hunters can cause lions to desert an area. For this reason some of the

A pride of lions has a leader who will drive away rivals and fight intruders.

hunters of the past who amassed huge totals of 'trophies' were relatively unsuccessful as lion killers. Similarly, lions slink away when a roving band of hunting dogs arrives on the scene. These dogs belong to a wild species and, although they are smaller and less powerful than lions, they are socially more highly developed and are better able to coordinate their attacks upon their prey. As hunters, many who know these packs of hunting dogs fear them more greatly than the big cats, and they have certainly been known to take on and overcome solitary lions.

Apart from disturbances of this kind, however, a pride of lions keeps to its own familiar territory. A pride seems to be basically a family group, consisting of a fully grown male and his harem, accompanied by cubs of various ages. A large pride may consist of thirty animals, but such a large unit is only likely to occur when game is exceptionally plentiful.

The chief male in a group does not easily tolerate mature rivals and may sometimes fight to the death with intruders. Young males are driven away as they grow up and often hunt for a while in small groups of three or four on their own. Probably because they must face the world on their own without the support and experience of the pride behind them, young males have a lower chance of survival than females. At birth the sex ratio of males to females is roughly equal, but in the Gir Forest of India, for example, there are four to five lionesses to every lion.

Lions and Man

Man has always both feared the lion as a source of danger to himself and his herds and respected the lion for its strength and bravery. Some people who are familiar with lions in the wild have argued, perhaps with some reason, that lions are not particularly brave, but simply are successful carnivores which have a well-developed sense of self-preservation and will flee from trouble as readily as any other animal. The fact remains, however, that the hunting lion, or even the frightened lion, often *seems* to be brave and this alone commands respect.

Man has thus two motives for killing lions: he can eliminate a troublesome predator, or alternatively he can overcome an exceedingly formidable adversary and thus enhance his own self-esteem. Primitive herdsmen could achieve both of these objects at once. It takes considerable courage for a group of men armed only with spears to surround a lion and wait for it to make an attempt to dash through the cordon to safety. However, for hunts of this kind the economic motive was probably the important one, and to this day some lion hunting takes on the aspect of pest control. Troublesome lions in India are usually killed by poison.

Lion hunting became popular as a sport at the beginning of the twentieth century, but it occurs much less nowadays. In the nineteenth century, big-game hunting was done mainly for profit.

With the invention of firearms, lion hunting became easier and rather less praiseworthy as a feat of arms, but the practice was continued as a sport. Some of the inhabitants of Abyssinia had to prove their manhood by killing a lion single-handed, shooting it at close range from horseback. The best-known European hunters in Africa in the nineteenth century had other motives and shot game largely as a business proposition. Lion hunting was therefore not of great importance to many of them, although it still took courage to use firearms that were liable to misfire and took some time to reload.

Lion hunting as a sport for Europeans became really popular at the beginning of the twentieth century. This was the period when a man disappointed in love was supposed—if he could afford it—to redirect his resentment toward the fauna of Africa. It was usually eastern Africa, for by this time the large herds of hoofed animals upon which wild lions depend had already vanished from other parts of the continent. This was the period when the successful hunter took pride in being photographed with one triumphant foot planted on the corpse of his victim.

Lion Taming

An alternative way in which man could show his superiority over the brute strength of wild beasts was to tame them. The idea is an old one, as the story of Daniel in the lion's den proves, and to this day the lion tamer remains an impressive figure. To most people, lion taming is one of those incredible feats which can be believed only if it is seen. That it can be done is obvious, but the precise scientific basis upon which it stands is a matter for argument.

What is involved may be all a matter of the distortion of ordinary social behavior. Animals which live in groups naturally have a relationship with others of their kind. They may, as a result of fighting or of bluff be of high caste, lording it over their fellows, or they may lose the contest and adopt a subordinate position. If forced into proximity with one or more mem-

A lion tamer gains the respect of his lions by bluffing his way into a dominant relationship with them. The relationship is a personal one; the lions would probably attack anyone else who entered their cage.

bers of another species, a social animal sooner or later starts to treat them as if they were members of its own kind. This sounds improbable, but we have only to reflect that a pet dog living with a human family speaks to them in dog language, wagging its tail or perhaps snarling, while its owners address it in their own tongue. Before long each party understands enough of the other's language for harmony to prevail. Ideally the pet dog should be in a subordinate position and do as it is told, but like any other social animal it will dominate its fellows if it can. We have all known examples of dogs which dominate their owners, who have put themselves at the disposal of their canine's every whim.

A lion tamer, then, insinuates his way into a group of lions, being accepted by them as one of their own kind.

The famous lioness Elsa, although a wild animal, became tame in captivity with Joy Adamson. They became good friends and Elsa always greeted Mrs. Adamson with pleasure, even when she later returned to the wild. Their relationship was a strong personal one and shows that animals should be respected for being what they are.

He can do it gradually, getting to know them while first protected by the bars of the animals' cage. Consciously or unconsciously he must learn to read the mood of each animal from the signals it makes, and at the same time he must impress on it that he is the superior animal. When the time comes for him to step into the cage, there must be no doubt. He must be dominant, and he must have established his position by bluff, for in actual combat he would certainly stand no chance at all.

On this basis the lion tamer uses skills of the same type as those used by a teacher, who is able to quell a rowdy class with a glance. In neither case is the physical strength of the parties particularly relevant. However, a lion tamer must be able to understand an alien language, and the penalty for failure is much higher than it would be in the classroom.

Undoubtedly showmanship plays a large part in lion taming. Risks must seem to be taken, but often the danger is greater in those parts of the act that look safer. The lions with which the tamer works will not all be equal in status. Some will have high rank and will be the leaders in the absence of the trainer. These individuals will be the most likely to attempt to enhance their status by taking on their only superior and must therefore be allowed no liberties. If these animals are kept in order the rest will give no trouble. With low-caste lions the tamer can safely afford to take more liberties, turning his back for long periods and at times encouraging them to snarl and appear more aggressive than they are.

It should always be remembered that 'tame' wild animals are never truly tame in the way that some domesticated animals are. Some domestic dogs, for example, are friendly to all people unless they are given very good cause to behave otherwise. No wild animals can ever be trusted to such an extent. When wild animals are tamed, it is in a much more limited sense. They are trustworthy with some people whom they know but would show no such respect for strange humans—any more than they would necessarily show respect to strange members of their own species. Behind the showmanship and bluster, a lion tamer must earn the respect of his lions and must respect them, in turn.

A tiger's stripes blend well with the shadows of tall grasses.

The Tiger—size and appearance

The tiger *(Leo tigris)* is almost the same size as the lion, to which it is quite closely related. Because of this there is no simple answer to the frequently asked question 'Which is the larger, a lion or a tiger?' They vary among themselves and it all depends which particular specimens one is talking about. Many tigers have been measured by sportsmen in the past, but not all of the figures given can be relied upon. For example, if you want to know how long the tiger that you have shot happens to be you can stretch it out and measure the distance between nose and tail tip in a straight line, or alternatively you can measure the same distance over the curves of the body, and this will give a higher figure for the same animal. If you skin it, stretch the skin and then measure it, you will obtain a still higher figure. Often we do not know which of these three methods was used in a particular case.

Probably the average male tiger is about as long as the average male lion—just under nine feet including the tail. It may be slightly lower at the shoulder than a lion, but if anything the body is more powerfully muscled. Certainly the tiger's back is slightly arched and looks stronger than the level back of a lion. Possibly the average tiger is the stronger of the two, but this cannot be proved.

That tigers are brown with black stripes is very well known, but few of those who have not had it pointed out to them realize that tigers have much white fur as well. In addition to white markings on the face and prominent white spots on the otherwise black backs of the ears, tigers are white with black stripes under the throat and body, and on the insides of the legs. This is countershading, a pattern which helps to cancel out the effect of shadows, making an animal appear to be flat and insubstantial. The tiger's stripes when seen in a zoo can give the animal a garish, yet beautiful appearance. The tiger has been well described as 'Death in a fancy dress'. Yet in the wild these same stripes blend well with the dark shadows of tall grasses or of the leaves of jungle trees.

The tiger is perhaps the most fearsome of wild cats to look at. Its brown and black striped coat camouflages it well in the wild.

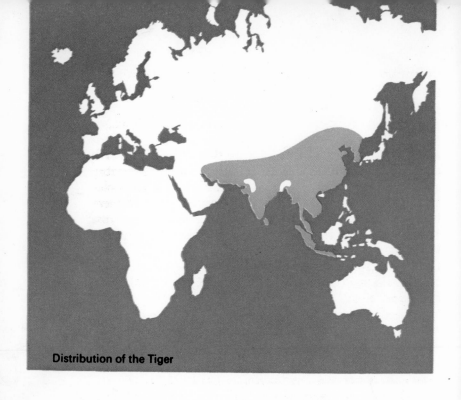
Distribution of the Tiger

The Tiger—range and variations in appearance

Tigers are often thought of as inhabitants of steamy tropical jungles. This is only partly true, and it seems likely that once it was not true at all. Fossils dating from some hundreds of thousands of years ago suggest that the ancestors of today's tigers lived in northern Asia, and from there the species has spread southward. Even today some tigers inhabit fairly cool parts of Asia, for the range of the species extends from central Asia and northeast China in the north, includes Persia, parts of India (but not Ceylon), Burma and the mainland of Asia, to the Malay Peninsula, as well as Java, Sumatra and Bali in the south. In most parts of this range tigers are declining in number, and those of Bali, for example, are rare. As usual, man is the culprit.

Although some tigers have lived in the tropics for thousands of generations, the species is still rather imperfectly adapted to the heat. The fur is thick, and it is very noticeable that tigers kept in zoos seem to revel in cold weather but dislike the heat. In countries where summer temperatures get very high, zoo tigers have been seen to immerse themselves in water so as to make a hot day more bearable.

It is only to be expected that a species with as wide a range as the tiger should show some variation in size and appearance in different areas. On the whole the tigers of the north are a paler brown than those of the south. This is presumably a matter of adaptation. In the less intense sunlight of cooler climates a paler color provides better camouflage. But there is no definite division between the lighter and darker forms. Just as the climate changes slowly as one moves from north to south, so the tiger population becomes slightly darker. Gradual adaptive variation of this kind occurs in many animals, and to describe it Sir Julian Huxley has coined the word 'cline'. Where a population of animals forms a cline, the typical animals from the extreme ends of the range may differ from each other considerably, but it is nevertheless difficult to divide the whole population into sub-species, for this means separating one group of animals from their very similar and closely related neighbors.

Similarly, tigers show a cline in the matter of size. Larger animals are found in the north, and smaller ones are found in the south. Once again this cline is adaptive, for larger bodies retain heat better than small ones do.

The striped pattern varies a great deal from one individual animal to another, but here, too, it is sometimes possible to distinguish between the inhabitants of different areas. With such a range of variation it is not to be wondered at that a number of subspecies of tigers have been named. Some of these, especially the island forms, are valid, clear subspecies which differ from their nearest neighbors.

Subspecies have a third scientific name added after those of the genus and species. Thus you will sometimes read of the Sumatran tiger, *Leo tigris sumatrae,* which is relatively small, very fully striped, has reduced white markings and a rather flat skull; you may also read of the Caspian tiger, *Leo tigris virgata,* from central southern Russia, which is medium-sized and has a long dark coat with many closely set brownish stripes. Many other examples could be given.

Wild tigers seem to be happy only where there is cover to hide them. They usually hunt by night, their dark stripes mingling with the undergrowth.

White Tigers

Of course, any population of animals can occasionally produce freak offspring, and this is what 'white tigers' are. One of the more common types of freak, found in many species, is the albino, which lacks normal dark pigments called melanins. White tigers are not true albinos, for they have some dark pigmentation, although only in a reduced form. They have dark brown stripes on almost white fur, ice-blue eyes and their noses and the pads of their paws are pink. White tigers have occasionally been glimpsed in the wild. In 1951 a young male white tiger was captured in the state of Rewa, India, and from this animal, mated to one of his own normally colored daughters, a number of white tigers have been bred in captivity, including the fine pair now to be seen in the National Zoo in Washington, D. C.

The Tiger—prey and hunting

Wild tigers normally live in remote areas where game is plentiful. Those of central Asia live among thick reeds or in bushes at the bottoms of river valleys. In summer they sometimes move to cover on higher ground, although they are never found above the tree-line in the mountains. In warmer climates tigers often inhabit mixed forest, preferably interspersed with rivers and outcrops of rock. They are sometimes also found in reeds and grass jungle where the vegetation may be over ten feet tall.

Although they are often forest dwellers, adult tigers rarely climb trees, probably because they are too heavy. Young tigers, however, quite often climb. Adults are usually solitary, although there are some reports of tigers hunting in pairs. They are mainly nocturnal, moving silently through the night in search of their prey. They can keep up a steady speed effortlessly and can easily cover fifty miles in twenty-four hours.

The prey hunted varies from one region to another. In Russia, tigers have been recorded as hunting wild boar, roe deer, elk, musk deer and even wolves. A wide variety of domestic animals are also taken when the opportunity arises, and these include dogs, cattle, horses, donkeys and camels. In the more southerly parts of Asia, tigers kill wild boar, deer of various species, antelopes such as nilghai and sometimes go in for even bigger game. It is estimated that in

White tigers (*right*) are extremely rare. They are not true albinos, which have totally white fur and red eyes, but their coloring is reduced below the normal range.

some parts of Burma one young wild elephant in every four is killed by tigers.

Tigers do not usually tackle full-sized elephants, for these may weigh between four and six tons and could easily crush a tiger. Even baby elephants are not easy meat, for the mother stays close by her young and is often accompanied by another female. For the tiger to be successful, the attention of both adults must be diverted before the young elephant can be killed.

In cases like this tigers usually get their prey on the move before attempting a kill, but against lesser opponents they more often steal in silently before bounding rapidly over the last few yards so as to take their prey by surprise. They sometimes kill by smashing the neck or skull of the victim, but they often make good use of their canine teeth, which are very long and powerful.

No doubt tigers' appetites vary, but it has been estimated that an adult tiger may kill in the course of a year about thirty victims, each with an average weight of 200 pounds. Obviously then, tigers eat meat when it is bad, for their kill will rapidly putrefy in the warmth of the tropics. Having made a kill, a tiger normally carries it off into thick cover, beyond the sight of thieving eyes, thus setting up a store of food which can be returned to again and again. A tiger in Burma once killed five bullocks, one after the other, and carried them off to form a really substantial larder. If anything, it almost seems that tigers prefer their meat partially decayed, and such is the tiger's strength that a bullock can be carried with ease.

When game is scarce a tiger will normally eat carrion. A dead buffalo, elephant or rhinoceros is very likely to attract its attentions, especially after putrefaction has set in. If even this source of food is absent, then the tiger makes for some other part of its vast territory, covering distances of up to 250 miles. The tigers that roam the most are probably those of the more northerly regions where game can be hard to come by, especially in winter.

The Tiger — breeding

There seems to be no particularly favored breeding season. Like other cats, the female tiger is in heat periodically and attracts the attention of males by means of her scent and her voice. The young are born after a gestation period of about 105 days, the nursery being any very secluded spot, such as a crevice among rocks or a cave, or in dense bushes or reeds. Up to six cubs can form a single litter, but between two and four is a more usual number, and not all of these cubs are certain to live for very long. Whatever size the litter was at birth, quite often only two youngsters survive to be weaned.

When they are just over a month old the cubs start to follow their mother as she hunts, although they are unsteady on their feet at first. As they grow, the area hunted by the family gradually increases, although they remain in the vicinity of each kill for several days. Eventually the young ones are able to play an increasingly active part in making the kill, but they do not become completely independent until the group breaks up, by which time they are between two and three years old.

In zoos tigers have been crossbred with lions. The offspring are known as *ligers* if a lion is the father, and *tigons* if a tiger is the father. Like mules they are usually sterile, but not invariably so.

Tigers attack large prey, such as a water buffalo, on the move, but they often approach smaller mammals stealthily, taking them by surprise. They use their long, sharp canine teeth to kill large victims.

Man–Eating Tigers

Of all the predatory mammals, the tiger has the biggest reputation as a man-eater, and this reputation is not entirely unjust. Some tigers do, indeed, kill and eat man. Naturally, these occurrences are not as common as they once were, because tigers themselves are less common, but in the nineteenth century 148 people in one year and 131 in another were reported as having been killed by tigers in Java alone. No doubt many such deaths went unrecorded, and as Java forms only a small part of the range of the species, it is reasonable to assume that tigers were causing far more deaths than, for example, air disasters do today.

It has been suggested that man-eating tigers are usually elderly individuals, who are too infirm for the pursuit of more active prey, and this may sometimes be true. Man, after all, is a fearsome animal in his own right and is very properly shunned by the great majority of wild animals. Only a desperately hungry tiger, it might be thought, would so far abandon caution as to hunt such an opponent. However, some suspected man-eaters when shot have turned out to be in their prime, and evidence as to their former feeding habits in the form of cloth or the skin from the sole of the human foot, which is very resistant to the digestive process, has been found in their stomachs, proving the case against them beyond all doubt.

Undoubtedly man-eating is a habit which is retained once it has first been acquired, for deaths due to tigers do not occur singly and sporadically. Once a man-eater gets to work the human inhabitants of quite a large area can understandably become terrified, as the roll of casualties mounts and the killer becomes bolder.

The first few victims may have been struck down as they moved unwarily along paths at night, but as the tiger gets more daring, acts of startling boldness follow. In nineteenth-century India, it was not unknown for soldiers to be carried off from their encampment, under the eyes of sentries. At about the same period at a place called Hurdwar, a tiger sprang from the concealment of a barley field in broad daylight, dashed in among the crowd and killed a trader who was peacefully occupied in chopping up spice.

Man-eating tigers are usually desperate, hungry animals. However, even when hunting is good, a tiger may not identify its prey as a man, and, having made as easy kill, become a confirmed man-eater thereafter.

The tiger was a wary and worthy opponent for hunters who enjoyed the thrills of danger.

Tiger Hunting

The activities of man-eating tigers drew the wrath of man down on them, but tiger-hunting was also a sport pursued for its own sake in colonial India. Two methods were used.

A buffalo, elephant or some other game animal could be killed as bait in an area known to be inhabited by a tiger. From a platform constructed in a conveniently situated tree, the sportsman could then keep vigil for several nights in the hope of a shot at a hungry, scavenging tiger. Some sportsmen preferred a more social and active method of hunting which could take place in daylight. The tiger was flushed from its daytime cover by a line of armed sportsmen mounted on elephants. This method was best employed in tall grass rather than in tree jungle. One such hunt in Burma a hundred years ago was well described by Colonel F. T. Pollok.

Pollok was hunting with some other officers when, in the middle of the afternoon, they received a message that a tiger was surrounded by beaters on elephants close by. Mounting his own elephant, Pollok was soon rewarded by

the sight of a charging tigress, which he shot at and wounded in the foot. Another shot had little effect and the tigress hurled herself at Pollok's elephant, which recoiled, throwing her off to the accompaniment of another fusillade, as a result of which she retired into cover. Again the hunters went after her, whereupon she sprang at Pollok's elephant, clinging to its face, mauling it with her teeth and claws.

In an effort to throw off his adversary for the second time, the elephant dropped to his knees, throwing Pollok to the ground with a gun still clutched in his hands. Picking himself up, he found it impossible to shoot at the tiger as it was too closely engaged with the elephant, and he therefore retreated to mount another elephant. This mount, too, was mauled as it advanced. Darkness was then closing in, and the sportsmen withdrew to tend the wounded elephants and a mahout who had also been bitten.

The following morning the tigress was found on her back dead, bearing wounds from thirteen bullets.

The Leopard

The leopard *(Leo pardus)* is another species with a very wide distribution in the Old World—indeed it has a wider range than any other big cat. In size it is smaller than either the lion or the tiger, but it is hardly any less redoubtable than its larger relations.

A good-sized leopard would have a head and body about 4½ feet long, and a three foot long tail. This makes a leopard only a little smaller than a lion—perhaps 18 inches less over-all—but the leopard is more finely proportioned, being not only shorter but also lower at the shoulder. A greater part of the leopard's length is made up of tail, and as a result it is very much lighter than a lion. Although leopards weighing 200 pounds or so have been recorded, most males weigh less than half this figure, and 70 pounds is a fair weight for a female.

The leopard's spots are clustered together, each cluster being called a *rosette*. There are no spots in the middle of the rosette. The brown fur is very much lighter on the under-

Black panthers (*left*) are in fact darkly colored varieties of normal leopards (*below*). They are not black, but very dark brown, and in bright sunlight the typical black rosettes of the leopard can be seen against this color.

parts, so once again countershading aids concealment. Like the other big cats, leopards have prominent markings on the backs of their ears, which are used as social signals.

Undoubtedly the leopard's pattern is camouflage, well designed to aid concealment among vegetation, and it is therefore surprising that leopards without this camouflage are not uncommon in some areas. As we have seen before, oddities can occur in any species, but if they are less well adapted than normal animals they will not usually survive to breed their like, and will tend to die out. It is therefore strange that unusually colored leopards are not rare.

The animals referred to are the darkly colored or melanistic leopards known as 'black panthers'. These are not members of a different species as is often thought. 'Panther' is simply an alternative name for the leopard and is quite commonly used in Asia for the species as a whole. Black panthers are simply leopards that happen to have very dark brown hair.

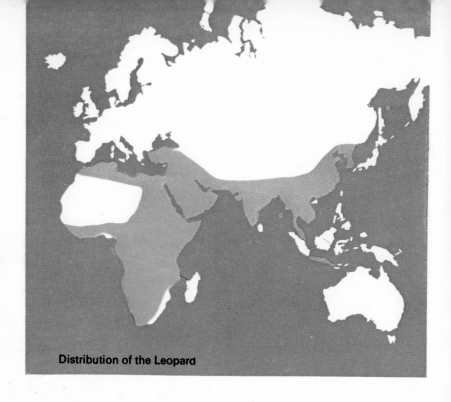

Distribution of the Leopard

Black panthers are most commonly found in the more humid parts of the leopard's range, and it has been suggested that the hereditary factors causing the dark color also adapt the animal to hot and sticky conditions, although it is not clear how they do so. As a black leopard is not so well camouflaged as its lighter brother (and both types can occur in the same litter), there must be some advantage they enjoy which would explain their survival in some numbers.

The Leopard—range

Leopards are quite widespread in Africa, although they have disappeared from the well-populated parts of southern Africa and are becoming quite rare in northern Africa. Elsewhere they are still numerous though their numbers are tending to decline, as they are shot for their coats which men or, to be more accurate, women covet. This is not a new trend introduced by Europeans, for there is in existence a ceremonial cloak from western Africa made from the skins of the tails of scores of leopards. Also just plain leopard cloaks were used by native Africans.

In Asia, leopards occur from Asia Minor in the west to China, Korea and Japan in the east. In the south their range includes India, Ceylon and southeast Asia as far as the islands of Indonesia. It is in India and southeast Asia that black panthers are especially common.

It would be expected that a species with a widespread distribution like this should show regional variation, but strange to say very little occurs. This is particularly surprising as leopards tend to stay close to their own territories and to breed with their neighbors, and as a consequence any one local population would be expected to be rather inbred. Such a breeding pattern is almost guaranteed to throw up local varieties and races, and yet with leopards this just does not seem to happen. Certainly a number of subspecies have been described and named, but there is little apparent difference between them, and a leopard from southern Asia looks very much like one from Africa.

Perhaps the most obviously distinct leopards are those of northern China which belong to the subspecies (*Leo pardus japonensis*. These are larger than average and have extra long fur. No doubt both of these features are useful adaptations to cooler climates. Chinese leopards are also particularly handsomely marked, having large rosettes.

Like tigers, leopards keep to the cover of thick plant growth whenever possible. In Asia, where the ranges of the two species overlap to a considerable extent, this does not mean that they are in competition to any marked degree. The tiger, by virtue of its superior size alone, is able to tackle prey that a leopard would choose to avoid, while the leopard has abilities which mean that it can succeed in hunting where a tiger would fail. Because of its lesser weight and graceful form the leopard is, for a big cat, an excellent climber. It can move along surprisingly thin branches, unseen by all but the most keen-eyed observer below. The branches also provide a refuge from danger and sometimes a peaceful sleeping place during the heat of the day. The long tail is valuable as a balancing organ when its owner climbs. Of course, it would be unreasonable to expect the leopard to be as superb a climber as the lighter, and very agile, monkeys, but for its size it is a very good performer.

In Africa, leopards are most common in bush country where the cover is good, but they sometimes also venture into forests. In tropical Asia they prefer the same conditions. Further north they seem to like inaccessible forests on the lower slopes of mountains, living at altitudes between 3,000 and 10,000 feet above sea level. Here they rarely descend to the foothills and are never seen on the plains, although they are common enough on plains elsewhere, as long as there is enough cover.

Even among the cats, leopards are exceptionally secretive. They are rarely seen unless they themselves choose to make an appearance, and they do most of their hunting under the cover of darkness. In rocky areas they often spend the day in the cool comfort of caves. Apart from courting couples and mothers with young, they are solitary by habit.

The Leopard—prey and hunting

At dusk, when it is hungry, the leopard starts to roam in search of its prey, moving wraith-like through the shadows. Once game is detected, usually by sight but sometimes by smell, it moves in softly and poises itself before springing to make the kill, usually by means of a bite which can easily crush the neck of the victim. Alternatively, the leopard sometimes lies in wait on an overhanging branch, coming down heavily on any animal that is unwary enough to pass below. It is difficult to obtain accurate figures for such happenings, but it is sometimes suggested that in Africa leopards kill more men than lions do, and if this is true it may well be the result of this habit of ambushing the incautious traveler. Humans may be attacked and killed before they are identified as such.

Leopards do not invariably leap for the throat of their prey. When attacking a substantial opponent such as a warthog, which is well armed with sharp curved teeth, a leopard will often prudently attack the hindquarters first, seeking to disable its victim before finishing it off.

Leopards hunt a wide variety of game. Antelopes, such as impala and waterbuck, are commonly taken in Africa, along with smaller animals like baboons (a favorite food in rocky areas), other monkeys and large rodents. Many travelers have written of the leopard's fondness for domestic

The leopard's prey consists of antelopes and deer, as well as baboons, monkeys and large rodents. The leopard often leaps at its victim from an overhanging branch.

119

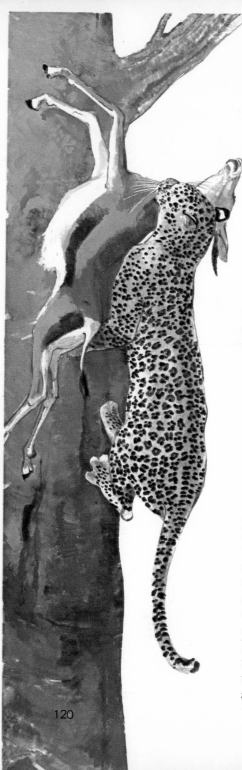

dogs, and wild African hunting dogs may come into the same category, as long as they are not part of a pack. In Asia, deer form an important part of the diet.

Having made a kill, the leopard, like the lion, first rewards itself by licking up any blood that has been spilled. The carcass is then dragged into hiding before being disembowelled. The entrails are buried in a shallow grave. The meal then begins with those delicacies that leopards appreciate most highly—the heart, liver, nose and tongue, followed by the haunch.

Long before morning, repletion is reached and then, if circumstances permit, the remains of the kill are seized bodily and, with a bound, carried up to a fork in a tree well above the ground and securely balanced. This habit of leaving the remains of the kill in a tree is a valuable one to the leopard, for it is thus removed from the reach of such nonclimbers as jackals and hyenas. No doubt the vultures and other feathered scavengers can get a share, but their appetites are relatively small. Like the tiger, the leopard may return again and again to the same kill.

Leopards often store
the remains of their
kill in trees.

The Leopard—behavior and breeding

Leopards are usually silent creatures. Females are sometimes
vocal when they are searching for a mate, but males may
give a coughing roar at any time. It is thought that they do
this for the same reason that birds sing—to establish their
presence in their territory and warn off intruders of the same
species. The voices of the other cats probably serve the same
function, except for the lion, whose roar may be a means of
keeping the members of the pride in touch with each other
rather than a warning and a threat.

Wild leopards seem to have no particularly favored breeding season. The gestation period is about 92 days. There are
usually between one and four cubs, three being the most
common number at birth, although it is rare for the whole
litter to survive to maturity. Adult leopards often breed
more than once during their lives and, as the number of
leopards in the world is declining, it follows that the chance
of survival of any particular newborn cub is not very high.
And if it is not going to survive to breed, an animal is always
most likely to die very young.

Children have been
carried off by leopards,
never to be seen again.

Leopards and Man

Apart from man, leopards have few enemies. In the wild
they die of starvation when food is scarce, from disease and
as a result of accidents. Drowning is unlikely to be included
in the last category for, like most other mammals, leopards
swim well, and have been known to reach islands in some
of the African rivers in this way. Colonel Stevenson-
Hamilton has described seeing a lion in pursuit of a leopard
on one occasion, and leopards certainly take to the trees
when a pack of African hunting dogs makes an appearance.

Leopards sometimes attract the wrath of man by carrying
off his domestic animals and sometimes, as has been mentioned, by making direct attacks on man himself. Because
of its secretive and nocturnal nature, a leopard can easily
remain concealed in the vicinity of human settlements,
obtaining easy prey and causing widespread terror. In Algeria
a hundred years ago, leopards were not uncommon, and
sometimes caused havoc among flocks of sheep and goats.
Men were less commonly attacked unless they provoked
attention. A cornered leopard is always very dangerous—
after all, even a rat will fight if it is cornered. During the day
it is always possible for a man to blunder too close to the lair
of a sleeping leopard.

Children are more likely to be attacked by leopards than are adults. Being smaller they may appear to be easier prey. More modern examples could be given, but let us complete the picture of nineteenth-century Algeria in this respect. A woman was working in a field, and she had left her baby on the ground nearby. It began to cry, and perhaps it was this that attracted a leopard which was lurking in a neighboring thicket. It dashed from cover, seized the infant in its jaws, and made off. The mother saw what had happened and set off in pursuit, but in vain, for she never saw either the leopard or her baby again. At about the same time in the same country, a boy of twelve was tending a herd of goats when he was attacked by another leopard, which wounded him so severely that he died of the injuries he received.

Leopard hunting

Because of the leopard's shy nature, nocturnal habits and its preference for killing its own food, the classic method of shooting leopards is to sit up at night, watching over a bait in the form of a tethered domestic animal, such as a goat. Some hunters keep vigil over the live goat, but this requires immense patience, for there is no guarantee that the leopard will deign to make an appearance. Bombonnel, a nineteenth-century French leopard hunter once spent thirty-four nights in succession in this fruitless manner. On the thirty-fifth night his luck changed and a leopard attempted to make off with the bait. Wounded by two shots, the animal sprang at the hunter and a desperate struggle ensued. Bombonnel was forced to let his gun fall, and was badly bitten about the face and left arm as he groped vainly for his hunting knife. At last, with a supreme effort he threw off the leopard and, picking up the knife, he staggered in pursuit. Fortunately for him, the leopard had made good its escape.

An alternative method of hunting is advocated by some other sportsmen. Once again a live domestic animal is tethered as bait. No further action is necessary until the leopard has made its kill. Being unable to drag the prey away, the animal will probably return to it, and this can provide the hunter with a chance. From a hide in a tree, preferably about thirty feet from the kill, he can then await his opportunity.

Colonel A. E. Stewart, a former officer in the Indian Army, has described his experiences of hunting in this way. Once in his hide he used to wait with his rifle ready from about three in the afternoon — the earliest possible time at which a leopard might be expected — until about 9 p.m. The leopard's approach, he says, was a silent one. Sixty yards from the kill it would halt and survey the surrounding area with suspicion. It might then take half an hour to cover the remaining distance, so great was its caution and so frequent the pauses. At this time the slightest move on the part of the hunter would send the quarry sprinting for safer cover.

Leopard hunting is carried out using a live tethered animal, such as a goat, as a bait for the leopard.

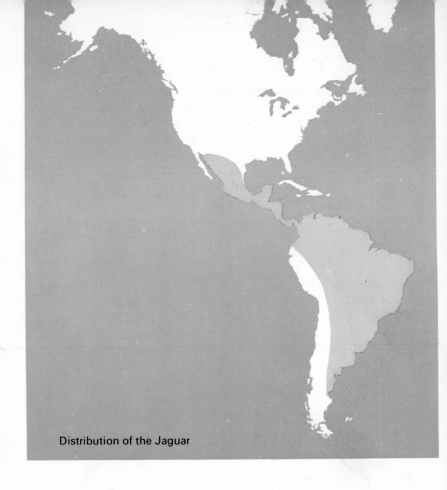

Distribution of the Jaguar

The Jaguar

The jaguar (*Leo onca*) is the largest of the cats of the New World. Only the lion and tiger are heavier. Although the jaguar was first reported at least as early as A.D. 1540 when the explorer Coronado came across the species in what is now New Mexico, relatively few jaguars have been weighed in the intervening centuries. One large male which was shot in Brazil scaled 290 pounds, and weights of over 200 pounds cannot be uncommon for males. Females are appreciably smaller and may weigh between 160 and 200 pounds.

At first sight the jaguar looks to be no larger than the leopard, being six or seven feet long overall, of which about two feet represents tail. However, in shape the jaguar differs considerably from its Old World cousin. The leopard is a graceful, beautifully proportioned animal, but those who know more about motor cars than they do about animals may be surprised to learn that the jaguar has a rather clumsy appearance. Certainly no member of the cat family can be downright clumsy, but the jaguar very nearly is. It has a rather large head, a tubby-looking body and a tail which is relatively short in proportion to the rest of the body. It walks, with a bustling, almost rolling gait. This characteristic alone makes it easy to distinguish between the two species in zoos.

Another method is to examine the pattern of the coat closely. Both species are spotted, and in each case the spots are clustered into rosettes of various sizes. However, leopards have no small black spots in the middle of each rosette, but jaguars almost invariably have one, two or more small additional spots there. Of course, it is only in a zoo or a museum that confusion between a jaguar and a leopard could arise, for leopards inhabit only Africa and Asia, whereas jaguars live only in America.

The jaguar's range extends from the southwestern United States southward to include Mexico, Central America and South America as far as northern Patagonia.

The jaguar is the largest American wild cat. Only the lion and tiger are heavier.

As is usually the case, slightly different types of jaguars inhabit different areas, and various subspecies have been described. The Central American jaguar, *Leo onca centralis,* for example, is said to be smaller than average. However, individual variation among a single population is often considerable.

One form of individual variation which is quite common in some areas is shown by 'black' jaguars which, like black panthers, are in reality very dark brown so that the darker rosettes scarcely show. Presumably melanistic animals like this are the result of a hereditary factor like that which causes red hair in humans, which tends to run in families. The jaguars of any one region will tend to be more or less closely related and will tend to resemble each other more closely than jaguars as a whole. Some years ago black jaguars were said to be particularly common in some parts of Costa Rica. Of course, as with the black panther, it is surprising that black jaguars, which are poorly camouflaged, should be as common as they are. There must be a reason, but we do not know what it is.

The name 'jaguar' comes from a South American Indian name for the species—'Yaguar' or 'Yaguara'—but throughout its range the jaguar is usually known in Spanish as 'el tigre', which obviously enough means 'the tiger'. Why this name was ever applied is another mystery.

The jaguar and the leopard are reasonably closely related species, being descended from a common ancestor that crossed a prehistoric land bridge between Siberia and Alaska. Once the connection between the continents was broken the two populations became more and more distinct until the present separate species came into being.

Jaguars are most often found in thick forests. Often they keep close to rivers in lowland areas where, in the tropics, the heat and humidity can be intense. However, in the Argentine they sometimes inhabit more open country, concealing themselves among reeds and thickets. In the southwestern United States, where jaguars have been very rare for many years, they have been reported in forested, rough mountain country about 9,000 feet above sea level. In Colombia, too, jaguars are sometimes mountain dwellers.

Jaguars are most often found in thick forest.

The Jaguar—breeding and hunting

In the northern part of their range jaguars are usually said to breed in January, but elsewhere they seem to have no fixed breeding season. Certainly in zoos, births may take place at any time of the year. The gestation period is between 95 and 105 days, and there are usually from two to four cubs, although exceptionally there may be only one. The young are at first very dark in color, for they are heavily marked with solid black spots which are only slightly paler at the center. Each of these spots later forms a rosette. As is normal in the cat family, the father plays no part in bringing up his offspring. They mature at about the same speed as the other big cats. One male which was hand-reared in an American zoo weighed 165 pounds at just under two years old and obviously still had quite a lot of growing to do at that age.

Jaguars hunt by normal feline methods. With care they stalk their prey through the undergrowth before launching

a final, lightning, close-range attack. Over short distances they can run swiftly, but they lack staying power. Sometimes they lie in ambush and wait for likely prey to pass close to them. They rarely launch an ambush from trees for, unlike the leopard, the jaguar does not take to the branches unless it is forced to do so in self-defense.

Jaguars hunt deer, large rodents such as capybaras and agoutis, the pig-like peccaries, and they are even said to tackle tapirs, which must weigh as much as fair-sized ponies. They are not narrow in their choice of diet, for they quite often eat fish which they scoop from the water with their paws and have even been seen to dive into the water in order to attack fairly large alligators. Despite popular belief, not all cats dislike water, and of course, most jaguars live in regions where the water is comfortably warm. On the beaches of Central America jaguars sometimes dig up and eat the eggs of turtles.

Jaguars swim with ease and often take to the water in pursuit of the capybara, a large water-loving rodent.

A jaguar is quite able to
swim whenever it is
necessary.

Jaguars and Man

As to the effect that jaguars have on domestic animals, reports differ. Some say that jaguars rarely kill man's livestock, but others give the impression that it happens not infrequently, and one jaguar in the southwestern United States killed seventeen calves in quite a short period.

There can be no doubt that as the numbers of men in the Americas have risen, those of the jaguar have fallen. In the seventeenth century, 2,000 jaguars were killed every year in Paraguay alone, but now, although jaguars are still far from rare in some areas, this would be considered a huge total in any part of the range of the species. Exactly how numerous jaguars are it is impossible to say, for they usually remain well hidden. Where the hunting is good they stay inside a fairly small territory, but when times are hard they roam widely, and at such times jaguars are likely to be seen in areas they do not usually inhabit.

Despite its size and undoubted strength, the jaguar rarely attacks man, and it is not as greatly feared as the other big cats. As an illustration of the jaguar's attitude to men the events near Center City, Texas, one night in 1903 provide a fair example. A party of boys out walking with their dogs discovered a jaguar, which promptly took refuge in a tree. One youth who was armed with a revolver shot and wounded it, and seeking safer cover it dived for the ground and took refuge in some bushes nearby. Here it was quickly surrounded by men who had been attracted by the commotion. Despite its desperate situation the jaguar did not indulge in any leopard-like sorties toward its human attackers. It mauled and killed one dog and meted out the same treatment to a horse which somehow became involved in the melee, but despite the confusion and the cover of darkness it made no attempt to attack any of the men before it was finally shot and killed.

However, one can never be quite sure how wild animals will behave, and occasionally jaguars have caused surprises. In 1825 a jaguar was living on a low, bushy island in a tributary of the Rio Grande in what is now New Mexico. The river became swollen by flood water and the jaguar had to swim for its life, coming ashore in the garden of the Convent of San Francisco in Santa Fe. Seeing an open door it sought sanctuary inside the convent where, entering the sacristy, it was immediately confronted by a lay brother (it was a convent for men) who was returning unexpectedly from confessions. The jaguar killed him, and afterwards killed three more men one after the other as they ran up to help. The survivors closed the sacristy door, imprisoning the man-killing jaguar. They then proceeded to make a loophole in the woodwork. Once this was completed, a gun was obtained and poked through, and the jaguar was shot before it could do more harm.

The Snow Leopard

The common name of the snow leopard *(Uncia uncia)* is rather misleading. It is not an ordinary leopard of any kind; and it does not always inhabit regions of perpetual snow. Big cats feed on herbivorous mammals, and no herbivore can get a living under such conditions. Besides, where carnivores do live among snow, as the polar bear is able to do because it feeds chiefly upon seals, they have white camouflage as is only to be expected. The snow leopard has some white fur, but it cannot be described as a white animal. No, the common name of this species is not particularly satisfactory. The snow leopard, because of its distinctive anatomy, has been placed into a genus of its own — *Uncia*.

There is an alternative common name, the 'ounce', but it rarely seems to be used these days. This may be due to the feeling that 'ounce' is rather a lightweight name to give a cat which is not only beautiful, but also quite large.

The head and body of a snow leopard together measure about 52 inches, and the tail adds another 36 inches to this total. At the shoulder the height is about two feet — about the same as that of some leopards. Perhaps the weight is about the same as the leopard's too — few snow leopards have been weighed, and it is difficult to be certain. As compared to the leopard, the snow leopard has a smaller head and the body looks longer in relation to the legs. Here the comparison is made difficult by the length of the snow leopard's fur which is only just over an inch long on the back, but which reaches a length of two inches on the tail and nearly three inches on the underside. Because of this extremely soft, luxuriant coat, the snow leopard appears considerably larger in body size than it actually is.

The winter coat is appreciably thicker than the summer coat, and is slighty grayer in tone, but the basic color is always gray-brown with perhaps a tinge of yellow in places. Countershading is present, so that the underside is almost pure white. The body is patterned with large black rosettes which tend to be rather indefinite in outline. The tail, which looks enormous because of the length of its fur, has dark markings. The backs of the ears are dark at their bases, but the tips are much lighter in tone.

The snow leopard's fur
is valued highly for its
warmth and is more
valuable than that of the
leopard. A few snow
leopards are trapped for
their fur in some parts of
Russia.

135

Distribution of the Snow Leopard

The Snow Leopard—range and breeding

Snow leopards are the least well understood of the big cats because they inhabit sparsely populated mountainous regions of central Asia. It is possible that there may be a few as far west as northern Persia and there may even be some in southern Persia, for it seems that perhaps they once lived there. Buffon, the famous French naturalist of two centuries ago, said that in Persia they were partly domesticated and trained for hunting, but perhaps he was confusing the snow leopard with the cheetah, which was often used for coursing (hunting). No other author seems to have referred to domesticated snow leopards, so there is considerable doubt.

Even today the range of the snow leopard is poorly known. It occurs in the mountain ranges of central southern Russia, such as the Pamirs, and from there eastward to Tibet and the Himalayas. Further north it extends to the Altai and Sayan Mountains and into Mongolia and into western China.

Although nowhere does it live in very northerly latitudes, the snow leopard lives at high altitudes and often encounters conditions which are cool or even downright cold. Accounts differ as to exactly how far up the mountains the snow leopard goes. One writer has mentioned an altitude of 20,000 feet in the Himalayas, but this figure seems a little exaggerated. A Russian zoologist who studied the species in Turkestan was probably nearer the mark when he said that it was usually found between 4,500 feet and 10,500 feet above sea level, with occasional forays to 14,000 feet.

Of course, like other mountain animals, the snow leopard migrates with the seasons, moving uphill during the summer and coming down for the winter, when it may even come down to 2,000 feet. In some areas it is said to live at this level the whole year round but even so, it must encounter some cold weather, for the interiors of large land masses have extreme climates, and there is no land mass larger than Asia.

The snow leopard is well adapted to resist the cold, for its coat provides excellent insulation and it has small ears, which are less likely to suffer from frostbite than large ones. Even the long tail—an appendage which is very liable to become chilled in some other species—is turned into an asset. When the animal curls up to sleep the tail is used as a perfect muffler to protect the bare nosetip.

The life cycle is also adapted to the climate. Tropical cats often have no very fixed breeding season, for to them all seasons are equally suitable for raising a family, but the snow leopard has a clearly defined breeding season. It would not do for the female to give birth to her young under icy, winter conditions. Mating occurs in late winter or early spring, and after a gestation period of 90 to 100 days the young are born in April, just as the days are getting warmer and the hunting is getting easier. There are usually from two to four cubs in the litter, and at first they stay in the den, often in a cave or a rocky cleft, although cases have been known of snow leopards making use of the huge nests constructed by vultures among the branches of low juniper bushes. By July the cubs start to follow their mother on her hunting trips, and they remain with her at least until the end of the following winter, when they are ready to hunt and find mates for themselves.

The Snow Leopard—prey and hunting

As might be expected from its spotty camouflage, the snow
leopard often hunts amongst the dappled shadows of the
juniper bushes and the spruce and birch forests on the mountain slopes. However, although the long tail would make an
excellent balancing organ there seem to be no authenticated
reports of snow leopards climbing trees to any marked extent.
Usually they inhabit more open country, lurking among
rocky outcrops on the fringe of the mountain pastures.

Snow leopards are sometimes active during the day, but
seem to do most of their hunting at night. Sometimes they
go after quite small game, such as birds, ground squirrels,
and pikas, which are related to rabbits, but they are capable
of tackling much larger prey. They kill deer and mountain
goats and sometimes manage to take gazelles by surprise in
the foothills. On occasion they will even take on the wild
boar, which is a very formidable opponent.

If game becomes scarce they may travel great distances
in search of it. Their migrations may follow quite a regular
pattern, for Ionov, a Russian observer, noticed that after a

Snow leopards often lurk among rocky outcrops, leaping out on to prey such as mountain goats and gazelles.

heavy fall of snow in winter or heavy rain in summer one particular snow leopard left its normal hunting ground and crossed a deep valley to reach another. A few days later, when the weather had improved, it returned by the same route.

Where their territory borders on pastures grazed by domestic flocks, snow leopards can become something of a pest for they frequently kill sheep, especially in winter when other game is scarce. They also take domestic goats and even cattle. In 1927 a snow leopard even succeeded in killing a horse belonging to the nomads of the Kirgiz Steppes of Russia, but this was a rare event. Horses are rather big game by a snow leopard's standards.

The method of attack used is either that of ambush or of stealing quietly toward resting or grazing animals. Quite often the last few yards separating the hunter from its prey are covered at a single bound, for snow leopards are superb jumpers. S. I. Ognev, a Russian zoologist whose word is to be credited, tells how he saw one clear a crevasse almost 50 feet wide.

Snow Leopards and Man

So far as is known the snow leopard does not attack man. At least, if it ever has no one has ever reported the event, which in some circumstances is a possibility, bearing in mind the lonely regions inhabited by this species of cat. However, without attacking man, snow leopards were once actors in a drama which has caused some excitement among the human population of the world.

For many years there have been persistent reports from the Himalayas of a strange creature which, from its description, is ape-like with human affinities. That these reports caused great excitement can well be imagined. The Yeti, or Abominable Snowman, caught the public's imagination. However, reports are one thing and concrete evidence is another. Apart from descriptions given by eye-witnesses—

Strange footprints found by explorers in the Himalayas and attributed to the 'Yeti' were probably bear prints.

descriptions which may have been garbled as they were passed on and translated—there were three additional pieces of evidence.

European climbers had seen footprints, made by what appeared to be bare, almost human feet, in the snow high in the Himalayas. One monastery had as a prized possession a hat, said to be made from the skin of a Yeti. And in addition to this there were strange roaring noises to be heard echoing round some of the high valleys.

An expedition went to the Himalayas to investigate and succeeded in borrowing the 'Yeti-skin' hat so that it could be brought back to Europe for investigation. The results were disappointing, for experts agreed that the skin was nothing like that of an ape and was probably that of a kind of Indian bison. The footprints also proved inconclusive, for although they could have been those of an ape or an ape-man they could equally well have been made by a bear—a much more likely possibility. But the roaring noises still required explanation. No known animal of the region was thought to have such a voice.

Now the snow leopard rarely roars and is, indeed, sometimes said never to do so. However, when angry it has a loud roar, as is only to be expected from such a big cat. Once this fact is known the evidence of the roaring could be explained. The snow leopard was providing the Yeti's voice.

So none of the evidence for the Yetis stood up to close examination, although this does not prove that the Yeti does not exist. Lack of evidence can never prove that.

THE CHEETAH

The cheetah *(Acinonyx jubatus)* is the oddest of all the cats and most certainly deserves its place in a genus of its own. Sometimes non-zoologists express doubts as to whether it is a cat at all but, although its running ability and methods of hunting are superficially dog-like, there can be no doubt that it belongs to the cat family. Even the method of hunting, when closely examined, turns out to be a variation on the cats' usual theme. Certainly the cheetah has evolved in such a way that it has come to be distinct from the other cats, but animals are classified by their ancestral relationships, and the cheetah evolved from the same ancestors as the other cats. It is not nearly as closely related to the dogs.

In its outline the cheetah is quite a large animal. The head and body are about 4½ feet long, and the tail another 2½ feet. At the shoulder it is sometimes three feet tall, but despite these dimensions the cheetah is very lightly built. The head is small and rounded, the jaws being much less strong than those of a leopard or jaguar. The

The cheetah is also known as the 'hunting leopard', a misleading name for it resembles the leopard only in being a spotted cat with a range that includes parts of Africa and Asia. Otherwise it is quite different. The adjective 'hunting' probably refers to the fact that cheetahs have been tamed by man and used as allies while hunting.

neck, loins and limbs are powerful, but slender. Like all animals, cheetahs show individual variation in weight, but the normal weight range of the species is between 110 and 145 pounds.

The fur of the cheetah is a rather light yellow-tawny shade and is marked with spots in a manner which is unique among the larger cats. It will be recalled that in the leopard and the jaguar the spots are grouped to form rosettes which may or may not have additional spots in their centers, depending upon the species. The jaguar has these extra spots and the leopard does not. In the cheetah the spots are not clustered into rosettes at all but are scattered equally on almost all parts of the body. Toward the end of the long tail the spots run together, forming complete rings which encircle it. The short ears have dark backs but are lighter toward their tips. A dark line runs from the forehead, through the eye, and down the side of the face. On the nape of the neck of both males and females there is a patch of longer hair, forming a small mane.

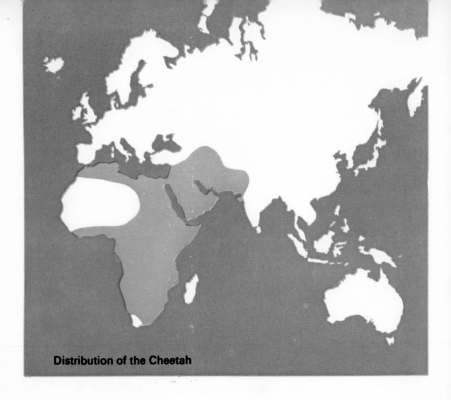

Distribution of the Cheetah

The Cheetah—range and subspecies

Formerly the range of the cheetah seems to have been much the same as that of the lion. It was found all over Africa wherever conditions were suitable, and also in the Middle East and a large area of Asia as far eastward as India. Today, because of the advance of civilization and the decline of the animals that it hunts, it has vanished from many of its former haunts.

In many parts of Africa, particularly in the north, it has become quite rare. Almost certainly it is extinct in Arabia and Jordan, and it has not been seen in Israel for over a hundred years. In India, it used to occur from the Ganges to the plains of the central Deccan, but none have been seen there since three were shot by one man in a single night some twenty years ago. The only cheetahs in Asia may now be in Persia, where there are perhaps a hundred of them; Turkmenistan in Russia, immediately to the north; and in Afghanistan.

144

The species is usually regarded as containing two subspecies, *Acinonyx jubatus jubatus* of Africa and *Acinonyx jubatus venaticus* of Asia, but there is no sharp difference between the cheetahs of the two continents. There is no agreement as to which of these two subspecies the few remaining cheetahs of Africa north of the Sahara should be placed in, and it may well be that they are of an intermediate type. If they are of the Asiatic subspecies it would not be altogether surprising, for the animals of northern Africa are in many ways more like those of western Asia than they are like those of the rest of Africa. After all, northern Africa is connected to Asia, and the Sahara Desert is a formidable barrier for animals to cross.

In 1926 a most unusual cat was trapped not far from Salisbury in Rhodesia. Its coat was not spotted but bore long dark stripes down the middle of the back and had exceedingly handsome, irregularly shaped dark blotches on the flanks. At first the animal was thought to be a hybrid between a leopard and a cheetah, but further examination proved beyond all doubt that it was simply a cheetah, typical in all except its markings. Inquiries soon brought to light the existence of other animals of the same type. At first it was thought that a new species of cheetah, named the king cheetah (*Acinonyx rex*), had been discovered, but nowadays these animals are regarded as unusually marked specimens of the ordinary cheetah species.

The king cheetah is an ordinary cheetah with unusual markings. It was discovered in Rhodesia in 1926. .

The Cheetah—prey and hunting

Cheetahs avoid both thick cover and mountainous areas, preferring open sandy plains or gently rolling landscapes. Often they inhabit arid semideserts where luxuriant vegetation cannot grow but where there is just sufficient rainfall to support some wiry grasses, which provide food for the cheetahs' prey, and a few stunted bushes which provide cover for the cheetah when hunting.

The prey is usually said to consist of fleet-footed hoofed mammals, such as Thomson's gazelle of eastern Africa, the goitred gazelle of the Middle East or the Indian blackbuck, but there is no doubt that cheetahs sometimes take smaller game. Sometimes they kill hares, and they do not consider birds as small as larks to be unworthy of their attention.

Unlike so many of the cats, they do all of their hunting during daylight. To avoid the heat of the day they are most active in the early morning and in the evening, but not before sunrise or after sunset. They could not operate successfully in the dark, for they need to be able to see their prey from a distance.

That the prey will not be close to the cheetah is almost inevitable, for gazelles and other inhabitants of the cheetah's territory seem to appreciate full well the risks attendant upon venturing too close to bushes, and they stay well out in the open. On sighting the prey the cheetah sometimes walks slowly but purposefully toward it, moving up-wind so that its scent does not provide a warning. Gradually it accelerates until it is hurling itself at full speed toward the potential victim. More often, however, it crouches, flattening itself and inching towards the prey before suddenly unleashing the final assault.

In either case the cheetah must be able to cover a considerable number of yards in a short time to achieve success, for the prey is wary and will be off at the first hint of danger. Some gazelles can run at fifty miles an hour and, if they have a reasonable start they will have every chance of escape. Indeed, they often do escape. Sometimes, though, the cheetah is lucky and, catching up with the prey, succeeds in bowling it over with a single blow of its paw. Alternatively, it may fly straight at the jugular veins of the throat, obtaining a death grip with its powerful jaws and teeth.

146

Cheetahs are unsystematic
feeders, often leaving
choice tidbits instead of
eating them first as a
lion or tiger would.

147

The Cheetah—running ability

In order to have any hope of success in hunting the cheetah must clearly be able to run faster than its prey and, indeed, it can do so. The cheetah is the fastest animal on four legs. Over short distances it can outrun gazelles, or if the opportunity present itself it could run rings round racehorses or greyhounds, for the cheetah can attain speeds of up to 65 miles an hour. However, its stamina is poor and it cannot maintain such a pace for many hundreds of yards. It is only a sprinter, and if it does not reach the prey within seconds it gives up that particular hunt.

When the cheetah's method of hunting is seen in this light, it becomes understandable. Like the other cats, it pounces upon its prey, but the conditions under which it operates force it to pounce from a distance, and this is why it has become adapted as a sprinter. It is the cat that springs the furthest.

Its light build and the length of its legs are adaptations for speedy running, and even the long tail provides a useful weight which can be adjusted during cornering if the prey twists and turns in a last effort to escape. However, it is remarkable that the cheetah should be able to outpace gazelles and blackbuck, for they, too, are adapted for running and are in one respect still more perfectly adapted for the purpose. In effect, hoofed animals run on their toenails, for that is what hoofs amount to, and along with this the leg becomes as long as anatomically possible. The cheetah runs only on tiptoe. It is not the perfection of its legs which makes it the fastest of all runners.

The secret lies in the waist region. In galloping a cheetah does not merely swing its powerful hind legs from the hip, but, by arching its back, it is able to swing them from the waist. This is the secret of its success. Studies of slow-motion film of running cheetahs have led one American expert to suggest that a theoretical cheetah with no legs at all could reach twenty miles an hour, humping along like a caterpillar.

As compared to those of other cats, the cheetah's feet are also adapted for running. Although young cheetahs can retract their claws to some extent, this ability is soon lost as they grow older. The adult cheetah's claws are permanently extended and enable the feet to grip the ground as they thrust the body forward.

The cheetah is the fastest animal, attaining speeds of 65 m.p.h. It gains its power by swinging its legs from its waist. It grips the ground firmly with permanently extended claws and with special pads on its feet that are ridged rather than rounded.

Cheetahs and Man

Of all the wild cats cheetahs are the most easily tamed. Cubs which are caught when young and comparatively helpless are likely to grow up to be reasonably docile, and even animals caught as adults can very often be tamed. It might be thought that to catch an adult cheetah would be a rare occurrence, but this is not so. The cheetah's lack of stamina makes capturing it a relatively easy feat. A man on horseback or nowadays, in a motor vehicle, can easily catch up with a cheetah.

Because it can be tamed and because of its speed, the cheetah has been used by man as an ally in hunting for many centuries. In India and Persia it was once almost commonplace for a wealthy potentate to have a string of cheetahs for coursing. One Mogul emperor in India four hundred years ago was reputed to own a thousand cheetahs

Hunters carried their cheetahs blindfolded to the hunting ground, unhooding and releasing them when game was sighted.

all at one time. It is not so well known that cheetahs were also kept in Russia, far from the present range of the species, and here they coursed game on the plains near the city of Kiev.

Cheetahs caught as adults were always found to be more efficient as hunters than young animals. Apparently the running ability of a cheetah is inborn, but its know-how in making a kill may be partly taught by its mother, and a natural upbringing is therefore most likely to produce a good hunter.

Sometimes the sportsmen were mounted on horseback, the cheetah being carried or conveyed in a special carriage with its eyes blindfolded. Once game was discovered the animal was unhooded and the prey was brought to its attention. When the cheetah saw the game, it stalked it carefully before making a final dash. If it was successful it was rewarded with food and blindfolded once more. As an alternative method of hunting, beaters drove the game toward a line of men with cheetahs which were released as the prey came into sight.

The cheetah was not the only cat to be tamed for the chase in India. The caracal lynx was sometimes used in the same way.

Cheetahs in Captivity

The cheetahs which are to be seen in zoos are quite often fairly tame. This is because they are usually specimens which were born in the wild, orphaned or abandoned by the mother, and taken into human protective custody while very young. Of course, they are not tame in the sense that domestic cats are. Although they can often be taken for walks on a leash or even with no restraint at all, they can be very stubborn and it is not unknown for them to sit down and refuse to be led anywhere. More than this, beneath a bland and apparently docile exterior they are still wild animals at heart. Their actions are never entirely predictable. For example, for a man to seem to run away from even a tame cheetah might be a great mistake. The sight of something behaving like the natural prey might well trigger off the normal reaction of pursuit. Even domestic dogs' behavior cannot be guaranteed in circumstances like this.

Although cheetahs are often to be seen in zoos they have always been regarded as the most difficult of cats to breed in captivity. That there should be difficulty is not surprising. Even lions, some of which have been bred in zoos for generations, do not always breed when they are expected to. There is more to it than keeping a male and a female in the same cage. Sometimes the conditions may not be quite right. Sometimes one of the pair may be sterile, or sometimes perhaps the animals concerned may just not like each other well enough to mate. Nevertheless, although disappointments occur, cats of most species breed reasonably freely in zoos. The cheetah has always been the notable exception.

The reason for this is unknown and this poses very many interesting problems. Despite their long history of association with man, cheetahs had never been bred in captivity until 1956, when a female in the Philadelphia Zoo in the United States gave birth to three cubs. They were raised to the age of three months before they died of feline distemper. In 1960, the Krefeld Zoo in Germany achieved the second success when two cubs were born. This litter was reared successfully, although bottle feeding was necessary. A few more cheetahs have been bred since then, but a litter of cheetahs is still cause for celebration among professional zoo keepers.

It may be that the limited success which has been achieved is the result of improved animal care, for the standards of the best zoos are continually rising. Perhaps diet is the most important factor here, for the first cheetahs to breed had been given a vitamin supplement in addition to their normal diet of meat. Other factors may be involved too. Research is beginning to show that for some mammals a natural upbringing for the young is essential if they, in their turn, are to make good parents. For the reasons already given, most zoo cheetahs do not have a normal start in life.

The gestation period of the cheetah is about 95 days. The cubs are born with their eyes closed—they open at just over a week—and at first a mane of long silvery-gray hair extends all the way down the back. This is lost at about ten weeks, although one tuft of longer hair remains on the nape of the neck throughout life. Until they are ten weeks old the cubs can retract their claws.

Cheetahs are sometimes kept in captivity.

WILD CATS AND ZOOS

In a way the animals in a zoo are ambassadors for their kind. It is true that we cannot see them doing all that they would do in the wild. The cats are not allowed to kill their own food, for example. If they did they would probably do it quickly and without fuss—the domestic cat is the only feline species to toy with its prey—but some of the public would hate the spectacle, and it is possible that one or two others would enjoy it too much. The meat is given already dead to zoo cats, and this helps most of us to keep up the pretence that meat-eating has nothing to do with killing. We like to keep butchery in the background, and we too easily forget that hunting is a natural way of life for some animals.

In every other respect, though, zoo cats lead lives which are as full and as contented as those of their wild relatives. It is true that they are not free to go where they choose, but this is only one freedom amongst others. They are free from starvation and fear and as free from disease as modern science can make them. Wild cats do not enjoy these freedoms. Zoo specimens on the average are larger, have glossier coats, and live longer than their wild relatives do.

Wild cats take exercise only when they must and spend much of their time doing nothing. Zoo cats take little exercise not because they cannot, but because they do not have to. In the large cages of some modern zoos the cats have room to run, but they rarely do. True, they pace up and down by the bars, but this is not an attempt to take exercise. Their one frustrated instinct is the instinct to stalk and to kill. The people beyond the bars become the prey, and the big cats move toward them as far as they are able.

No, zoo cats are not free to kill—few would suggest that they should be—but otherwise they are content. Often their contentment shows. They purr as often as wild cats do. And we, restricted in only slightly different ways by the restraints of our civilization, can see them and understand them better, and thus understand better the living world of which we are a part.

The pacing of a caged tiger is an attempt to stalk prey.

BOOKS TO READ

There are a few books that are solely concerned with wild cats. These include:

Cats of the World. Armand Denis. Houghton Mifflin, 1964.
Born Free. Joy Adamson. Collins, 1964.
The Bobcat of North America. Stanley P. Young. Stackpole, 1958.
The Puma, Mysterious American Cat. Stanley P. Young and Edward A. Goldman. Dover, 1946.
Simba. C. A. W. Guggisberg. Chilton, 1963.
The World of the Tiger. Richard Perry. Cassell, 1964.

Most general and regional books on the distribution and habits of mammals include information about cats. Some titles of this nature are:

Mammals of North America. V. H. Calahane. Macmillan, 1947.
Biology of Mammals. Richard G. Van Gelder. Scribners, 1969.
The Natural History of Mammals. F. Bourliere. Knopf, 1954.
A Field Guide to the Mammals. W. H. Burt and R. P. Grossenheider. Houghton Mifflin, 1952.
The Mammal Guide. Ralph S. Palmer. Doubleday, 1954.
Wild Animals of North America. The National Geographic Society, 1960.
The Book of Indian Animals. Stanley H. Prater. Bombay National History Society, 1943.
Animals of East Africa. C. A. Spinage. Houghton Mifflin, 1963.
Mammals of Eastern Asia. George H. H. Tate. Macmillan, 1947.
Mammals of the U.S.S.R. and Adjacent Countries. S. I. Ognev. Israel Program for Scientific Translations, Oldbourne, 1962.
The Terrestrial Mammals of Western Europe. G. B. Corbet. Foulis, 1966.

PLACES TO VISIT

Wild cats can best be seen in game reserves in their countries of origin. However, most people are only able to see these animals in zoos. A few of the zoos where these very popular animals can be seen include:

Bronx Zoo, New York City
Staten Island Zoo, New York City
Franklin Park Zoo, Boston, Massachusetts
Philadelphia Zoo, Philadelphia Pennsylvania
National Zoological Gardens, Washington, D.C.
The Brookfield Zoo, Chicago, Illinois
San Diego Zoo, San Diego, California
San Francisco Zoological Gardens, San Francisco, California
Crandon Zoological Gardens, Miami, Florida
Cincinatti Zoological Gardens, Cincinatti, Ohio
Milwaukee County Zoo, Milwaukee, Wisconsin

Many of the rarer and sometimes already extinct varieties or species can be seen only as museum specimens. Museums where exhibits of recent cats, fossil cat ancestors and cat anatomy can be seen include:

American Museum of Natural History, New York City.
United States National Museum, Washington, D.C.
Field Museum of Natural History, Chicago, Illinois
Carnegie Museum, Pittsburgh, Pennsylvania
Milwaukee Public Museum, Milwaukee, Wisconsin
Los Angeles County Museum, Los Angeles, California

INDEX

159

OTHER TITLES IN THE SERIES

The GROSSET ALL-COLOR GUIDES provide a library of authoritative information for readers of all ages. Each comprehensive text with its specially designed illustrations yields a unique insight into a particular area of man's interests and culture.

NOW AVAILABLE

PREHISTORIC ANIMALS
BIRD BEHAVIOR
WILD CATS
FOSSIL MAN
PORCELAIN
MILITARY UNIFORMS, 1686–1918
BIRDS OF PREY
FLOWER ARRANGING
MICROSCOPES & MICROSCOPIC LIFE
THE PLANT KINGDOM
ROCKETS & MISSILES
FLAGS OF THE WORLD
ATOMIC ENERGY
WEATHER & WEATHER FORECASTING
TRAINS
SAILING SHIPS & SAILING CRAFT
ELECTRONICS
MYTHS & LEGENDS OF ANCIENT GREECE
CATS, HISTORY—CARE—BREEDS
DISCOVERY OF AFRICA
HORSES & PONIES
FISHES OF THE WORLD
ASTRONOMY
SNAKES OF THE WORLD
DOGS, SELECTION—CARE—TRAINING